DESEED THE LEMON

*ELEVATE YOUR PERSONAL BRAND
...ONE PIP AT A TIME*

DESEED THE LEMON

ELEVATE YOUR PERSONAL BRAND
...ONE PIP AT A TIME

KELLY LUNDBERG

ISBN: 9798882612411

Imprint: Independently published

Copyright 2024, Kelly Lundberg

All views expressed in this book are those of the author and are not intended for use as a definitive guide. This work is owned in full by the primary author, Kelly Lundberg. No part of this publication may be reproduced or transmitted in any form what soever without the written permission of Kelly Lundberg: info@kellylundbergofficial.com

This book was edited and produced with with Write Business Results Limited. For more information on their business book and marketing services, please visit www.writebusinessresults.com or contact the team via info@writebusinessresults.com.

WRITE BUSINESS RESULTS

ACKNOWLEDGEMENTS

There is an old African proverb: "It takes a village to raise a child." To everyone in my village, without whom I'd not have had the support, encouragement and insights that has taken **Deseed The Lemon** from pen to paper and then to print… I love you and I thank you!

All books begin with an idea. That idea needs to be a good one, with a clear sense of who the reader is. I wrote my first draft of **Deseed The Lemon** in the spring of 2019, sitting at a friend's kitchen table. I was back in the UK on one of my visits to take part in a business masterclass. That's where it stayed, on the table, an idea needing work and so did I.

Fast forward to 2023, I was ready to reignite my passion for storytelling and this is where my path crossed with Georgia Kirke, founder and director of Write Business Results. This meeting immediately re-fuelled my desire to tell this story and gave me a feeling of purpose to share my narrative. She made me believe that I had something to say and so to Georgia and Ivan, thank you for being with me every step of the way, and to Katherine for my many edits.

There were moments where there was little light at the end of this tunnel, moments where Graham's unending patience and reassurance gave me the push to keep going. To mum for her hours spent reading and deciphering my "creative" but often jumbled thoughts, and to dad, who is my biggest social media supporter (just ask the algorithms). To Mhairi, chief proofreader and a huge support, thank you all.

Thank you to my coaches and mentors, there are many in my village. Blake Sergeant and Denis Liam Murphy who always encourage me to own what I do. Blake, you've enabled me to articulate the vision of **Deseed The Lemon**, slice by slice. Denis, for opening the door to me understanding myself, believing in the possibilities and potential and the power in being truly honest with myself.

To Irish, my right-hand woman, who manages to turn the messiest of my scribbles into knock-out content. And my extended team, for all your support and hard work in helping move this project forward.

Friends help celebrate good times and provide support during bad times. The value of friendship builds lasting roots and is one of the best gifts life has to offer. When you find it, hold on to it.

Acknowledgements

Sarah and Yvonne, thank you for the endless hours of practical and emotional support and for always having my back. Natassia, thank you for keeping me accountable and smiling through our daily workouts, a big reason I've had the energy to get this book over the line; and to Tash, who knew that our chance meeting on the red carpet over ten years ago would turn into such a fabulous friendship.

Granny, without your slices of lemon (no pips, of course) in hot water, there may never have been a book at all. I feel sure you are looking down on me, smiling over what started with your simple wisdom which has resonated with me ever since.

To my clients, without whom there would be no book. They have entrusted me to share their personal brand messaging and successes. The truth is that building a memorable personal brand is a journey, not a destination. It's about identifying unique strengths and consistently showing up as the best version of yourself, and they do this by deseeding the lemon each day.

I have loved working with you and seeing first-hand how you have all grown, forging credible and inspired personal brands. Nothing makes me happier than following your social media, features in magazines, podcasts and book publications. Your wins are phenomenal, congratulations.

To my audience, those who've joined us recently and especially to those of you who have been with me over many years, thank you.

Deseed The Lemon

My goal is to inspire you to deseed the lemon, act now and take the first steps on your own journey. Tell me and the world your story…

CONTENTS

Acknowledgements	I
Preface	1
Introduction	9
What is a Personal Brand?	23
Slice One: Strategy	**33**
Auditing – Where Are You Now?	36
Where You Need to Go	49
Pitch to Profit	71
Slice Two: Style	**85**
Why Style Matters	90
Never Trust a Man in Crocs	104
The Substance Behind the Style	123
Slice Three: Stationery	**139**
What is Stationery and Why it Matters	142
Strike a Pose	172

Slice Four: Social   **191**
How Social Are You?   194
Hirebarbara.com   216

Slice Five: Spotlight   **231**
From Air Hostess to Author   233
Think Big Picture   252

Slice Six: Speaking   **263**
One to Many   266
Getting Speaking Gigs   284

Slice Seven: Stand Out   **297**
Ways to Stand Out from Everyone Else   299

Conclusion   323
About the Author   329

PREFACE

"GIVE A GIRL THE RIGHT SHOES, AND SHE CAN CONQUER THE WORLD."

— Marilyn Monroe

As soon as I slipped my feet into those exquisite, crystal-embellished, tiny size 35½ Jimmy Choo sandals, I knew they would be coming home with me. You know that giddy rush you get just before you're about to make a purchase? The kind that you **so** know you can't quite afford, yet still find a way to justify to yourself? Yes, **that** giddy rush. It swept over me, and I felt that heady rush of excitement and trepidation, all mixed up together.

OK, so my new shoes are not quite magical enough to help me stride out there and take over the world, and despite their crystal perfection, they can't guarantee me a Cinderella experience and bag me a Prince Charming. In fact, they're going into my bag at a price, one that will cost me dearly, as I know it will be the proverbial beans on toast for the next month or so. But what a girl needs – what **this** girl needs – is that paradisaical pair of shoes!

I know myself very well; shoes have always been my weakness. Their call of temptation is like that of a siren. Despite that, don't think for one moment that those Choos were a shallow buy. The thing is, even as a young child, shoes have always been my nemesis. Small feet mean limited choices, so when you get a pair that fits, you buy them.

For you, it may well be a bag, a banging dress, the latest Gucci belt or that car you always aspired to own that gives you your own personal moment of shopper's satisfaction. Or, like me, a well-fitting pair of well-made shoes.

Buying my first pair of Jimmy Choos was one of those fantastic, memorable experiences for me. One where I can remember every detail of the moment, down to the outfit I was wearing, what it felt like to clutch that shopping bag in my eager hands and stride out of the store (so, so good). Likewise, I feel the same sort of nostalgia towards the memory of that moment when I opened up and read my first, good, non-fiction book about life and business, and the eager anticipation I felt as I turned those pages.

Reading **The Magic of Thinking Big** by Dr. David J. Schwartz was life changing. Every word seemed so obvious, so simple, so logical to implement. These were actual steps, written down for me, showing me how to implement

Preface

change in my life by setting high goals and then exceeding them. The realisation that I could do what I was reading was an absolute game changer.

At the time, I was working as cabin crew for Emirates Airlines. It was a dreary wet day at London Heathrow departures, and I had just finished reading the book and couldn't get it out of my mind. I was determined to use what I had read to challenge myself. Facing me was a seven-hour flight with 357 passengers on board, and I was determined to make every moment of the trip count, and make sure the passengers had an outstanding experience. How, though, was I going to achieve this? Keep it simple, I thought. I'm going to smile at every single passenger with more enthusiasm and greater energy than I had done so before. Sounds pretty manageable and effortless—obvious, even—so why hadn't I ever applied this practice intentionally before?

"TAKE INTEREST AND EVEN DELIGHT IN DOING THE SMALL THINGS WELL."

— Jim Rohn, entrepreneur, author, and motivational speaker.

Call it a coincidence, or perhaps it was the cause-and-effect of the recycled air at 35,000 feet, but the energy on that flight was electrifying and my eyes were truly opened to everything around me. I was hooked on the high that came with the knowledge that it takes so little effort to make so much of a difference in someone else's life, as well as my own; this approach to life and to everything I do was something I could get behind. So now what else could I learn or do that would have a meaningful influence not only on me, but also create a ripple effect on others around me as well?

Reading a book, listening to a podcast or a webinar, going to a workshop or attending an event are all ways in which to enrich one's mind, and I began doing them all with gusto. The magic begins when you take action and you make things happen. Doors begin to open, opportunities begin to appear, your reality begins to change. Does a great pair of high heels help? They can't hurt! Just as long as you know that you can conquer anything the world throws at you.

Gradually, I began to realise that I wanted so much more out of life. Whilst I was doing well, and was actively seeking out ways to improve myself, both professionally and personally, I needed to embark on a new challenge. Cue the call of the fashion world. I have always wanted to be a stylist, long before I even knew it was a profession you could get paid for. I worked in retail from a very early age, and my favourite part was making recommendations for customers and helping them find their style.

But my love for styling had to go on hold for a little while, and my career took a different path. When I turned 22, I moved from Edinburgh to Dubai in the United Arab Emirates, a relatively unknown place at the time, to take up a flight attendant job, which felt like a dream come true;

Preface

I was getting paid to see the world in style and wouldn't have to resort to stuffing my Choos and all my beloved belongings into a backpack. If you haven't figured it out yet, I'm not exactly the backpacking type. Sure, I had no idea where Dubai was on the map and had to look it up, but I couldn't wait to see what my travelling life had in store for me.

Arriving in the city and getting to know it was a heady experience. A melting pot of cultures, a mecca for holidaymakers, a business hub and a haven for entrepreneurs, Dubai was and still is the most vibrant city in the world, clearly on the rise with an almost tangible buzz in the air that nothing is impossible. Dubai proves this mantra time and time again, whether through its man-made island shaped like a palm tree, the biggest indoor, real-snow ski slope complete with its very own family of penguins, the dancing fountains at the foot of the tallest building in the world, the largest aquarium to be found inside a mall, or the city's newest landmark – the Dubai Canal waterway – with its very own waterfall. Dubai knows how to create experiences, and taught me that I could create an experience out of everything I did too.

Even at the earliest stage of Dubai's dynamic growth, and even with all my dreams and passions, I could not have imagined that so many of my clients would include the celebrities, royalty and the uber wealthy of the city. Some of these clients were living in the world's tallest building, the Burj Khalifa with its 163 floors, while others were guests of the 7-star Burj Al Arab hotel. It is one of the more luxurious locations where I love to sip my cups of hot water and lemon—more on that later! The can-do nature of Dubai's visionaries and the people who had chosen to make this city their home was contagious, and I had caught the bug.

In 2005, while living in Dubai, I left my job as cabin crew to start making those dreams a reality. With my resignation accepted, I set out to launch the Middle East's first personal shopping and styling service. In Dubai, anything is possible, and I believed it wholeheartedly.

But how did I go from being a celebrity stylist, to building Brand YOU Creators, the leading personal branding agency in the UAE and working with some of the biggest brands, sports stars and entrepreneurs in the world?

Well, first, I fell in love with books.

> *"START READING, AND ESPECIALLY READ THE KINDS OF BOOKS THAT WILL HELP YOU UNLEASH YOUR INNER POTENTIAL."*
>
> — Jim Rohn, entrepreneur, author, and motivational speaker.

Preface

It's fair to say that I came to reading books a little later in life than some. My English teachers would despair of me in class. One even told me that I would never be of a calibre to achieve good grades in English, and not to even think about taking higher English (which is the Scottish equivalent of an English A-level). Wrong! Tell me what I can't do, and I'll prove to you I **can** do it; does that sound at all familiar?

I actually passed my higher English in the one year, and you can imagine my teacher's amazement when I presented him with a copy of my first book, **Success in the City,** ten years later. But that's another story, for another time.

Books have changed my world as they have done for countless others who choose to further their experiences and expand their learning. My goal is that this one leaves a lasting impression on you and **Deseed The Lemon** becomes a new way in which you embrace life and everything you do.

Think big. Always think big. Now let me explain what I mean when I say let's deseed that lemon.

Deseed The Lemon

INTRODUCTION

I don't drink coffee, I never have. My day always starts with a cup of hot water with a slice of lemon, preferably in a bone China mug or cup. My choice is often met with people expressing their opinion and a fair share of incredulity, "No coffee? How on earth do you function in the morning?" I just smile.

Don't get me wrong, you may find me at some point during the day with an occasional camomile tea, or one of my other vices, usually the alcoholic kind; a glass of rosé wine (my first preference – always) followed closely by a skinny bitch (vodka, fresh lime, and soda), but that's not ever first thing in the morning. As far as my other weaknesses go, there is my small addiction to shoe shopping. Never has it been a cup of coffee.

Why hot water with lemon? I attribute my liking for and drinking of it to habit. For as long as I can remember, every morning, my Scottish granny would religiously retrieve her favourite China teacup, boil the kettle, and pour hot water over a fresh slice of lemon. She did this every day of her life.

Granny I found was very fussy about her preparation of the perfect cup. Hot water, but not too hot, and a slice of lemon which she always cut with a sharp knife with all the pips carefully removed. Her words still ring softly in my ears, "Kelly dear, there's nothing worse than having your hot water and lemon spoiled by a few pips floating around your cup."

Over the years spent at home and during my many travels, I've developed the very same habits when it comes to drinking hot water and lemon, including the fussy part. It's amazing how something so simple can be spoiled when that attention to detail, of deseeding the lemon, is missed. Believe me when I say that I've lost count of the number of restaurants and hotel lobbies where I have found myself ordering hot water and lemon, and what has been delivered definitely wouldn't meet my granny's standards.

Here's the thing, it's a relatively simple drink to make, or so you would think, and one that can easily be served up pretty much anywhere. Whether it's made in a McDonald's, a Michelin 3-star restaurant, a 7-star hotel or a hotel located in the African bush, a cup of hot water with slices of lemon can arrive in various shapes and forms, very often far from perfectly formed. Even the most prestigious hotels can make a momentous mistake (like leaving the pips in) when dispensing a cup of hot water and lemon!

Introduction

How, then, do we make the perfect cup? In my experience, it really is quite simple. It's all in the attention to detail. From my years of working in fashion and now in personal brand strategy, attention to detail has been my everything. In all that I do I like to think that I go the extra mile, to make sure that every client experience is exceptional and memorable. I realised quickly that not all things are created equal.

It's the small things that can separate out the average from the excellent. The accumulation of seemingly minor decisions or actions can easily be overlooked by others. The more I thought about that cup of hot water and lemon, the more I reflected on the act and effect of deseeding the lemon. By going over and above, and with just a little extra effort to find the right cup and deseed the lemon, the perfect production can either be lifted to a whole new level or sunk to a new low.

It's become my metaphor, deseed the lemon, a phrase I find myself applying to all that I think and do. Reflecting further my thoughts crystalized; deseed the lemon could become a valuable tool that would work, professionally and personally, not just for me but for others too.

Throughout this book, you will not only find my personal experiences of deseeding the lemon, but also the inspiring stories of my clients and friends. In Chapter 7, you'll hear Barbara's journey as she unexpectedly went viral online, ultimately leading to her landing a brand-new job. And then there's Winnie, who shares how she managed to secure her dream PR feature in the prestigious pages of **Vogue** magazine. These real-life life examples, plus many more, serve as inspiring testaments to the transformative power of deseeding the lemon.

Choosing to adopt these principles and incorporate elements into your own personal branding strategy provides the fundamental elements that will enable you to set yourself apart and determine how you communicate your message to the world. Whilst my clients' backgrounds, beginnings and status of careers are all different, each has found value in the understanding of the Brand YOU Creators formula, which utilises seven key "slices" I'll share shortly that are the foundational pathway to building and elevating personal branding success.

Why you need a personal brand

We live in an increasingly digital age. We can no longer rely on just having a presence on social media platforms; it's about crafting a cohesive and authentic image that represents who you are and what you stand for. Personal branding is more than a series of random experiences, it's about building a personal brand that stands out which means an exploration of strategies to showcase expertise and unique qualities.

But I know that putting yourself out there can be scary. Often what holds people back from actively working on their personal brand strategy is the fear of criticism or negative feedback. You will need to step outside your comfort zone. Self-disclosure can, however, lead to closer relationships and a better shared understanding with the

Introduction

people you meet. It forms a crucial part of developing your public brand.

It will require you to challenge your mindset and adjust your thinking, setting clear goals, seeking guidance or mentorship, and taking consistent action. Building a personal brand is not just about promoting oneself, but also about sharing valuable insights and experiences, connecting with others and creating meaningful relationships in the professional world.

Your knowledge, great or small, can help someone. You are in fact doing a disservice by not sharing how you can help them. Think less about you and your fears, think more about how you can help others. The more you choose to share, the more you can determine your authenticity with your audience.

We can all be the world's best procrastinators. Lack of time and the perceived complexity of various social media platforms, content creation and networking, not to mention feeling overwhelmed with professional and personal commitments, can make it challenging to allocate time to personal branding efforts. It can, however, all be achieved, and with great success, by following a creative plan. The key is to slice your plan up to make it manageable.

SLICE ONE: STRATEGY

Building a successful personal brand begins with defining a personal brand strategy. It requires clear thinking to craft a unique value proposition. It means taking stock of the now, identifying strengths and weaknesses, understanding target audiences and setting clear goals of where to go next.

GET THE BUILDING BLOCKS RIGHT AND YOU WILL STAND OUT FROM THE COMPETITION.

Introduction

SLICE TWO: STYLE

Personal style is an essential component of a personal brand. It's not just about what we wear, but also how we communicate, our body language, and the overall impression we make on others. Crafting a personal style that reflects our unique personality ensures we can succinctly enhance our personal brand.

IT'S NOT JUST ABOUT THE TALK, IT'S ABOUT LOOKING THE PART.

SLICE THREE: STATIONERY

Creating professional and visually appealing collateral is essential. It is a tangible asset that affects how others perceive us. The influence of a personal brand extends far beyond physical appearance and communication style.

Culture is driven by beautiful imagery, stunning professional photography, a striking website, an attractively scripted email signature, good-looking business cards, and eye-catching promotional materials. These all play a critical role in shaping our branding footprint.

YOUR VISUAL BRANDING DRIVES THE MIND OF THE CONSUMER.

Introduction

SLICE FOUR: SOCIAL MEDIA

Love it or hate it, social media is here to stay. A cohesive digital persona will boost credibility. An online presence is very often the first impression people will have of our personal brand; content should be designed to get others excited about our messaging as we interact with our target audience. A crucial component in today's digital age, social media allows us to build credibility and trust with others.

BE AUTHENTIC AND TRUE WHILST PRESENTING A PROFESSIONAL IMAGE.

SLICE FIVE : SPOTLIGHT

Media and PR opportunities are powerful tools for building a personal brand and increasing our visibility, providing the spotlight to allow us to step out from among the crowd. A bold and recognisable image will resonate with others, it will capture other people's attention. Pursuing media opportunities is our platform to gain tangible traction for showcasing our expertise and unique qualities.

BE RECOGNISED EXTERNALLY FOR WHO AND WHAT YOU ARE, AN EXPERT IN YOUR FIELD.

Introduction

SLICE SIX: SPEAKING

To mobilise a personal brand, public speaking and presenting are crucial. The spoken word is more powerful than the written. Through storytelling we can share ideas that will travel further and have greater impact.

Vision is what people will follow. Therefore, fashioning engaging presentations and delivering them with confidence and authenticity is the culmination of the experience, skills and values that differentiates one individual from another.

LEARN TO LISTEN AND EARN THE RIGHT TO BE HEARD.

SLICE SEVEN: STAND OUT

This is where you can truly deseed the lemon and stand out. It is the accumulation of seemingly minor decisions, actions and characteristics that, when combined, shape a distinctive and compelling personal brand. Without a personal brand you quite simply are part of the many, and not part of the few.

Your personal brand is your currency, so build equity. It's in our power to appeal to our audience and fashion the image we wish to project to appeal to our chosen audience. Standing out is a magic elixir, a unique selling point (USP).

Building a strong brand is like building a house, we can't build without strong foundations, so get your "slices" right! It takes time, effort, and a clear methodology. Think of building a personal brand like having a long-term savings plan, which will require consistent effort. Every action, no matter how great or small, compounds over time and yields bigger results, whether that's growth in wealth, reach, reputation, or influence.

Introduction

A personal brand is a necessity and no longer can be seen as a luxury, as I'll show you in Chapter 1. Having a personal brand that authentically represents who we are, and that captures people's attention, will elevate our abilities, and allow us to achieve the personal and professional goals we desire.

DESEED THE LEMON AND ELEVATE YOUR PERSONAL BRAND …ONE PIP AT A TIME.

Deseed The Lemon

Chapter 1:

WHAT IS A PERSONAL BRAND?

Something I hear a lot from people I meet for the first time at speaking events, as well as potential clients, is that they don't want their business to be about them or that they want their work in the organisation they work for to speak for itself. But the truth is it's their DNA and their experiences that are so often what makes their business so special, or their contribution to a business special, and the reason why people want to do business with them.

It took a phone call from luxury retailer Harvey Nichols back in 2009 for me to understand I had a personal brand and was so much more than just my business name. The marketing team were looking for a host to present a styling workshop post their twice a year fashion show. The team wanted to bridge the gap after their glitzy, high-end off-site fashion show and share how the fashion trends from the runway could be translated into easy, wearable day-to-day looks.

It was a dream opportunity at that time in my career, working with fashion designers and a marketing and PR team who had big ideas. I not only picked up new clients, but felt part of a fashion family for years which, when you own a small business, can be priceless. It was also a big deal and a clear sign that my credibility and business was moving in the right direction. The opportunity was also paid which made it feel even more official. As instructed, I sent my logo, high-resolution images and my bio to the team, who then proceeded to let me know that they couldn't use any of it.

Initially I panicked and straightaway thought perhaps my pictures were not good enough quality or that they did not like my logo. Thankfully I didn't have to wait too long for the team to reply. Their response was, "We work with people not businesses, we want to have YOU not your business in store and we need your own name and logo." That's when the aha moment happened.

People buy from people they know, like and trust and this was no different. I quickly set about the task of creating my personal brand guidelines, more about this in Slice Two, set up a website and really began to understand the power behind your own brand name while building a business.

From research I've done over the years, Tom Peters coined the term "personal branding" back in 1997. An article published by **Fast Company** under the title "The Brand Called You." he said:

> "START RIGHT NOW: AS OF THIS MOMENT YOU'RE GOING TO THINK OF YOURSELF DIFFERENTLY! YOU'RE NOT AN 'EMPLOYEE' OF GENERAL MOTORS, YOU'RE NOT A 'STAFFER' AT GENERAL MILLS, YOU'RE NOT A 'WORKER' AT GENERAL ELECTRIC OR A 'HUMAN RESOURCE' AT GENERAL DYNAMICS (OOOPS, IT'S GONE!). FORGET THE GENERALS! YOU DON'T 'BELONG TO' ANY COMPANY FOR LIFE, AND YOUR CHIEF AFFILIATION ISN'T TO ANY PARTICULAR 'FUNCTION'. YOU'RE NOT DEFINED BY YOUR JOB TITLE AND YOU'RE NOT CONFINED BY YOUR JOB DESCRIPTION. STARTING TODAY YOU ARE A BRAND. YOU'RE EVERY BIT AS MUCH A BRAND AS NIKE, COKE, PEPSI, OR THE BODY SHOP."[1]

So, whilst the idea of personal branding isn't new, I do feel in the post-pandemic world that the marketplace is more

---

1   Tom Peters, (1997), 'The Brand Called You', *Fast Company*, 31 August, available at: https://www.fastcompany.com/28905/brand-called-you

crowded. You can work remotely, be hired as a speaker for a company in the USA, and not leave your apartment in Dubai. But people want more. They want transparency and authenticity from the people they work with or people they hire, and they want to know the story behind the brand. It is often why, on average, employees have ten times more followers than their company's social media accounts and content shared by employees receives eight times more engagement than content shared by brand channels.[2]

Your personal brand is the amalgamation of both your online and offline persona, and specifically how it is perceived by others.

How do people feel when they come into contact with something you say or do?

The last part brings it back to deseeding the lemon.

I've discovered over the past six years of helping people create their personal brand strategies that often they don't actually think they have a personal brand. If I ask "Who already has a personal brand?" at a speaking event, it's met with a response of half hands up. I hear things like, "I sort of have one." Or "I don't have one and I'm working on it next year." To be clear, a personal brand is not reserved solely for CEOs or celebrities – it is something that everyone has, whether they realise it or not, and regardless of

---

[2] Erskine, R. (2016) '22 Statistics that prove the value of personal branding,' *Entrepreneur*, 13 September. https://www.entrepreneur.com/starting-a-business/22-statistics-that-prove-the-value-of-personal-branding/280371.

your job title or level of fame or influence; your personal brand can have a significant impact on your business, career and personal life.

One of the most common myths about personal branding is that it's only for outgoing or extroverted people. Many people believe that only those who are comfortable promoting themselves, or have a large social network, can build a successful personal brand.

However, this is far from the truth. Personal branding is not about being the loudest or most visible person in the room. It's about understanding who you are, what makes you unique, and how you can communicate your value to the world.

Here are a few reasons why personal branding is not just for outgoing people:

1. **Authenticity matters:** A strong personal brand is not about being someone you're not. It's about being true to yourself and communicating your values and strengths in an authentic way. This means that introverted or reserved individuals can build a personal brand that reflects their unique qualities, and still be successful.

2. **Different communication styles:** Personal branding is about finding the right communication style that works for you. Not everyone is comfortable with traditional networking events or speaking on stages to thousands of people, but there are many other

ways to deseed the lemon and build your personal brand.

3. **Niche expertise:** Many introverted or reserved individuals have deep knowledge and expertise in a particular field or industry. Personal branding can help you communicate that expertise and establish yourself as a thought leader in your area of focus.

4. **Building relationships:** Personal branding is not just about promoting yourself – it's also about building relationships and connecting with others. Introverted or reserved individuals can still build strong connections with others through one-on-one conversations, building relationships online or participating in smaller group settings.

Another confident statement I have read or heard people say over the years is, "I've done my logo and my brand is complete." While a logo is an important visual representation of your personal brand and first impression, it's only one part of the overall picture to be discussed in Slice Two.

A further misconception is that creating a social media profile means you have a personal brand. It is not just about creating a flashy online profile or accumulating a large number of (fake) followers. Personal branding and deseeding the lemon one pip at a time is about creating a positive impression that reflects who you are as a person, and what you stand for. It's about being authentic and transparent, and this can only be achieved by consistently demonstrating your values and character through your actions and interactions, both online and offline.

What is a Personal Brand?

Personal branding involves developing a reputation that precedes you. It's about positioning yourself as an expert in your field, someone who is trusted and respected by others. This requires not only creating content that showcases your expertise, but also actively engaging with others in your industry, not just being a voyeur online. So while social media is an essential tool for personal branding, more of this in Slice Four, it is only one aspect of a much more comprehensive and nuanced process. By understanding the true essence of personal branding, you can take control of your professional identity and build a reputation that will serve you well throughout your career.

The aspect that most people find hard in the beginning of their personal brand journey is understanding that as much as a personal brand is about you, it's not only about "you". It's about finding the balance between promoting yourself and providing value to others. It's about you and your audience. You're not just shouting about what you've done, you're sharing your knowledge and helping others solve problems. You're creating engaging content and participating in conversations that matter. When you bring all of this together,

you can establish yourself as a thought leader and build a community of like-minded people. You're promoting yourself and your brand while giving back to your audience and helping them in their personal or professional lives.

By providing value to your audience, you build trust, credibility and authority in your field, which can lead to new opportunities, collaborations or partnerships. In this way, building a personal brand is not just about you, it's also about the impact you can have on others and the world around you. Personal brands in the fitness industry, on social media for example, have managed this well by providing and sharing knowledge of workouts to their followers.

You want to create a name for yourself that stands the test of time. Personal branding is not a one-time event, as I mentioned in the Introduction, you have to think of your personal brand being like a long-term savings account. It's an ongoing process of cultivating your skills, expanding your knowledge and building your network. It's about being intentional with your actions and decisions and creating a brand that will continue to grow and evolve as you do.

In order to get the best from this book, I want you to know that nothing you try is a failure and when you take massive action it might be far from perfect (we know by now perfect doesn't exist). Your social media post might not get the visibility you wanted. Your first speaking gig might bomb. Your first lead magnet might not convert, I could go on… But that's what taking big leaps feels like, and it's only when you look back you can join the dots.

Not everything will go to plan, and not everything will get the results you're looking for. At the time, you might even feel as though you've failed, but that's OK because you've still taken a step. What often happens is that when you look back on how far you've come, you'll realise that even the "failures" helped you make progress. So, don't let the fear of taking a leap hold you back.

What is a Personal Brand?

This is your time to take your personal brand to the next level, play a bigger game, and become a better person. Lose the stories of your past that you are not "techy", you don't have time for yourself or think no one will listen to you. I want you to realise that what is obvious to you is amazing to others. You have been called to this book because it appealed to you. You are ready and you want to transform your personal brand, so now that you better understand what your personal brand is, let's dive into the first Slice – Strategy – so you can lay strong foundations and build your personal brand to last and open doors to new and exciting opportunities, for you and your business.

Deseed The Lemon

SLICE ONE:

STRATEGY

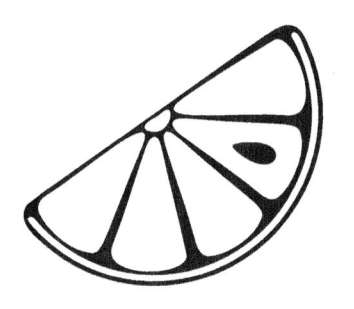

Creating and maintaining your personal brand requires strategy, intentionality and consistency. It's the same concept that applies to anything that you want to do, and do well. Putting thought into and actioning what you want from life requires planning! So many people take days, weeks and months to plan big life events. Think how many hours you may have invested in planning your dream holiday, your special birthday or your wedding. Imagine how powerful it could be for you if you invested the same time and effort into your personal brand, business or career growth.

Building your strong personal brand requires foundational elements: authenticity, your point of view, consistency, storytelling, expertise and networking. Essentially it is your road map.

Your personal brand strategy, when well thought out, will drive a strong and credible personal brand. It all starts when you set defined goals and actions. You need a strategy that is articulate at the outset. Every strategic plan starts with vision; with every step you take, your vision becomes more and more tangible as you work through a considered process.

For some, your desire may well be to establish yourself as a thought leader in your industry, which means that you will need to focus on creating valuable content and building a strong online presence. Perhaps you are looking for a new job or career advancement. Or you may be considering launching a new business. If these are your goals then you need to start sharing elements of your journey. Creating valuable content, building a strong online presence, storytelling, networking and showcasing skills and expertise are all powerful tools. They go a long way to establishing authority and driving growth, and will only add to your personal brand.

However, before you start creating any strategy, you need to know where you're starting from, otherwise you risk directing your focus to the wrong places. Even if you've never actively worked on your personal brand before, trust me when I say you have one. So, that's where we'll start – by auditing your current personal brand.

Chapter 2:

AUDITING – WHERE ARE YOU NOW?

"YOU ARE WHO GOOGLE SAYS YOU ARE."

A friend calls you up to ask if you're up for a blind date. She gives you a rundown – his name, job, how she knows him. You laugh and reply, "Why not?" Your friend passes on his number and you organise to meet him. But you don't really want to go in truly blind so you decide to do a little of your own online research.

Here's my question to you, "What would you think if you couldn't find anything about the person you are planning to meet online?"

Whether you have gone on or would go on a blind date is immaterial. I always find this entertaining to ask when

Auditing – Where Are You Now?

I am working with my clients, even if it's a hypothetical conversation. Would you or would you not use the internet to "Google" for more specific information about the person you planned to meet? The majority of those I ask do admit that they would do a little proprietary research.

But what happens when there's nothing to be found? Would you wonder how genuine the individual or individuals are, or more precisely what they could be looking to hide? Perhaps they are catfishing, a deceptive activity in which they have created a fictional persona or fake identity. The internet can be a fishy place!

Of course, you would "Google" – and you wouldn't be alone. Google search is very often the first place people will look for information that is published about you.

Don't get me wrong, some individuals, positions and companies may require a level of discretion, but for the majority having some sort of digital representation adds to their credibility and helps them articulate clearly who they say they are.

Whether you're considering signing up with a new client, or getting a company to represent you, you are very likely to seek out information to make better-informed decisions. We all want to know more about the person or persons we engage with either personally or professionally.

So, the next question is, what does Google say about you?

When I run a masterclass, I get all the attendees to "Google" themselves. They find out all sorts of things!

Some discover they don't even exist online; while others learn the only images of them online are very outdated and no longer represent how they look. One attendee even found a photo on a Pinterest board showing him with a pina colada with an umbrella in it in hand, yet confessed he wasn't sure he had ever even used that platform. Someone else found an unflattering article. Of course, it's not all bad – others are pleasantly surprised and want to capitalise on their new-found online presence.

What do you find when you "Google" your name?

Google offers us quick, fast, and easily accessible information and ideas. It's a popular search engine and one that is a go-to for many.

Whether you are a recruiter looking for a new candidate or a client about to purchase a service online, you will more than likely use Google to see what's being said about a person or their personal brand.

So, when was the last time you checked yourself out with Google? When I say you, I don't mean your business. Some of you may or may not have a business profile, what I am talking about is you. Take a pause here and search for yourself. Why? Because you need to know what's out there to manage your online reputation.

What happens when you hit Google search? You may already have a community presence, perhaps a personal branded website or a profile on LinkedIn, the world's largest professional online social network. LinkedIn runs as a search optimised engine and is where you will more than likely find the first visible link about you on the internet, or if not LinkedIn then one of your other social media platforms.

When you're locating your presence on the internet, it's always wise to undertake an audit of how many times you appear. Whilst there's no rule of thumb for this, with my clients I recommend they scroll through up to three Google pages. Even if you can find no visible evidence of you existing with your front-page Google search, it's still important to see what lies beneath. You never know where you might find a little gem hiding; after all, with more and more personal information shared on the web, you never know where your name could pop up on an article or blog post.

Check Google images too. What appears, if any? The web is a big place, you never know what images can find their way online, some of which can show you in a less than positive light. I can remember one specific occasion where just this happened to me.

A journalist from a well-known newspaper in Dubai asked to interview me at home. The article also required visuals, and they arrived with their press photographer. The interview went well; the photo shoot, however, did not.

As can often happen on home shoots, lighting, space and clean backgrounds can prove challenging for even the best photographer. No matter their skill, if you don't connect or feel the part, this will transcend into your visual representation.

The article went to press, without me realising that nothing flowed. The lighting was off, my outfit didn't flatter, my hair and makeup didn't match the mood. The backdrop was far from calm. Whilst the article itself was on point, the photograph that ended up on the web was not. When I "Googled" myself, the offending photograph always popped up; it didn't even look like me – perhaps that was a blessing, it really wasn't a good visual at all!

It wasn't until I was working with one of my clients and demonstrating the importance and value of a Google search that I popped up yet again. A perfect reminder for me to remove the image, held on the website, along with any others that I felt no longer represented my personal brand. Small gains can be easy to achieve – by contacting the content publisher that photograph no longer has an online presence. You just never know if something is possible, until you ask.

Check Google videos too. Video content is a great way to build credibility, it's where you can showcase your style and get your audience connected to the authentic you. There is nowhere to hide with video content. Content can find its way onto various platforms, corporate channels, YouTube or even TikTok. Making valuable checks could lead to you finding that a copy of last year's Christmas dance that you wished you hadn't performed has found its way onto the web. Your personal brand will evolve. Misinformation, false representation and outdated content can damage your brand, either personally or professionally, so you need to regularly audit your presence and remove anything that no longer serves you.

Auditing – Where Are You Now?

My Google search unearths a great number of hairstyles not to mention colours – let's just say some were not my finest moments. As a celebrity stylist, my career spanned well over 15 years. It was, and still is, a creative and colourful industry where you can express yourself as individually as you wish, and it rarely affects your personal brand. I had all shades of hair colour from pink to purple. In fact, so much so, on one of my trips to LA, California, I found myself sitting with a cup of hot water and lemon in a corner café on Santa Monica Boulevard, when David Beckham drove by in his Range Rover. Stopping at the lights, he looked over, rolled his window down and called across, "I like your hair." Fluorescent pink hair certainly got me noticed. It worked to enhance my personal brand in those days.

I grew up in the '90s. One of the biggest priorities then was to keep my Tamagotchi alive.[3] We didn't have to worry about high school party pictures and inappropriate fancy-dress outfits being posted on Facebook. No tweets, blogs or selfies to look back at and regret. Certainly, there was not the pressure there is now when friends and family, albeit naively or unwittingly, can freely tag you in unwanted posts – they will rarely ask for your permission to post. The internet has become a bit of a free for all and you just never know what you can be exposed to.

---

3   For those too young to know what a Tamagotchi is, they were virtual pets, in the shape of an egg on a key chain – perhaps we could consider this an early iteration of AI.

The same goes for any other third-party content. If you find something you don't like or feel it misrepresents your brand, find the website owner's contact information and send them a request to remove it, much like I did with my offending photograph.

If you can't find anything on Google that relates to you, that's not uncommon. You could undertake a more in-depth search using your name plus modifiers, like a known nickname, a city in which you live or have lived, the names of your school(s), further education or companies you have worked for or still do. If you still find nothing, use further modifiers, such as your business name, to see if anything shows up and more importantly needs to be removed.

Take some time to evaluate what you see and work out what needs to be removed first by yourself. Some easy successes could be achieved by going through your social media platforms to identify anything that might portray you in a less than positive light. It can be a lengthy process sifting through outdated content. On some occasions, where you cannot invest or have not got the committed time, you could consider burying the content within Google, however, to do so you have to highlight positive brand content. I'm an advocate of you doing this right and doing it right the first time, often the best outcome is not to opt for the short cuts! Therefore, I would recommend taking the time to go through that outdated content and remove what no longer serves you.

If in doubt, always look to remove content where you have discontinued a product or service and where you have changed prices significantly. You may have changed location, your contact information or even sold your business, if that is the case these are all triggers for you to remove or update content. One of the worst violations is when you find someone impersonating you online, promoting your content and sharing false information. This is a serious offence. In cases of copyright violation, at the time of writing, you can submit a Google DMCA Takedown Notice.[4]

Google is a powerful user reference point; it uses algorithms which determine what you will see when browsing the web. Far be it for me to walk you through the complex details, other than to say that algorithms sift through billions of pieces of content that are in Google's index. Algorithms look for phrases and keywords that match your query.

If you have a business it is a good goal to be on the front page on Google search results to stay ahead of the game and get noticed. Whilst there are hundreds of factors to determine the ranking of relevant search results, positive content ranks highly.

Your personal brand strategy means you will need to be constantly creating new social profiles and publishing fresh content. This also goes a long way when it comes to you looking to bury any negative search results you may find.

Content can be varied, it can be personal or professionally related, as long as it is authentic and value driven. Take

---

[4]   https://reputation911.com/google-dmca-takedown/

hobbies as a great example. I am often asked to write articles for online publications to which I have currently, no personal or professional affiliation. I just like to share what I see as fun information that you can enjoy, learn from and test the waters with too.

One such article I wrote was for **Raemona**, an online women's magazine. It was called "I love rebounding and here's why", which quite unexpectedly turned out to be one of the most read articles **Raemona** has posted. Just like me, you too will have stories to share that will spark interest and could contribute to enhancing your Google spotlight. You will need to find a way to keep tabs on your online reputation and keep abreast of anything that comes out in your niche.

TOP TIP: SET UP A GOOGLE ALERT FOR YOUR NAME

To stay on track, set up a free Google alert for your name. Here's how I set up mine:

Visit Google.com/alerts. In the search bar, type what you want Google to alert you about.

Click "Show options" to change settings for frequency, sources, language and region. You can also specify how many results you want and where you want them delivered.

Click "Create alert" to start receiving alerts on yourself or other search topics you're interested in – think keywords in your niche and include your own name.

You can take it one step further; I created a free download that can support your personal brand audit. My personal brand mastery has a checklist that highlights collateral you may be missing and key points to consider when strategically building your personal brand. You'll find a link to access it in the Resources section at the end of this book.

In summary, a personal brand audit of what's available on the web about you is essential, it gives you a valuable opportunity to optimise existing content and remove anything that no longer serves you.

What do other people think of you?

For clients who wish to dig deeper into their personal brand, we will often explore the perception that others have of their perceived personal brand. This requires them to approach people who know them well and will tell the truth. Feedback can come from several sources – a trusted confidant or confidante, a coach, colleagues, even family and friends. There are two main rules:

1. It requires absolute honesty!

2. It's always done anonymously.

I ask these people to answer the following six questions:

1. What five words come to mind when you think about [name]'s personal brand?

2. How would you describe [name]'s personal style? (e.g stylish, polished, creative, well-groomed, classy, sloppy, dated, overdone, ill-fitting, inappropriate, unrefined).

3. What do you consider [name]'s strongest personality traits to be? (e.g reliable, confident, adaptable, optimistic, creative, genuine, supportive).

4. What are some areas that [name] could improve in when it comes to their personality traits?

5. How would you describe [name]'s overall communication style?

6. How does [name] come across on social media?

Opinions will always vary and do, but this is a valuable exercise to identify any blindspots you may have. Despite all our efforts we all possess blindspots about how we present ourselves which ultimately impacts our personal brand. It's good to be curious. Working with our blindspots and openly embracing them, provides a positive environment, restoring a commitment to grow and keep our vision fresh.

Acknowledging blindspots means a greater self-awareness, space to identify areas for improvement, and a valuable insight for refining your personal brand strategy, communication and online presence.

DESEED THE LEMON, ONE PIP AT A TIME

KEY PIP TAKEAWAYS

GOOGLE YOURSELF AND SEE WHAT COMES UP.

REMOVE ANY UNWANTED OR NEGATIVE CONTENT.

CREATE YOUR STRATEGY TO REPLACE UNWANTED OR NEGATIVE CONTENT WITH NEW, POSITIVE CONTENT.

SET UP A GOOGLE ALERT TO STAY IN THE KNOW WHEN CONTENT ABOUT YOU IS RELEASED.

Chapter 3:

WHERE YOU NEED TO GO

"I AM A PUBLISHED AUTHOR WITH A THREE-BOOK DEAL."

Goals, the bigger, the better! You can, literally, take your pick of thousands of books written about goals. Of those books you may choose to read, each one will have a different perspective on how to set goals and achieve them, personally or professionally.

Clarifying your goals enables you to set a direction for your future. They can be big or small, ambitious and as lofty as you wish. Ultimately, they are your way to help you align your focus to promote a sense of self-mastery.

As a self-titled goal queen, I love setting out personal and professional goals and am equally passionate when working with my clients to help them to find their voice and amplify their message. This can be achieved by good goal setting.

"YOU MUST TAKE PERSONAL RESPONSIBILITY. YOU CANNOT CHANGE THE CIRCUMSTANCES, THE SEASONS, OR THE WIND, BUT YOU CAN CHANGE YOURSELF. THAT IS SOMETHING YOU HAVE CHARGE OF."

— Jim Rohn, author of Seven Strategies for Wealth and Happiness

---

Goals give you direction, help you to identify what's important to you and keep you accountable. Well-thought-out goals will help you to prioritise your time, measure progress and ultimately increase productivity.

Goal setting is quite simply a process to think about the future and what you want. How you are going to get to where you want to go takes planning and you might not have all the answers at the time for the "how" part, and that's OK. So, how do you incorporate goals as part of your brand strategy?

Where You Need to Go

Ask yourself, what is your "why"? What is your overall purpose and why? What are you trying to achieve and why? After all, why do we get up in the morning? Why do we go to work? Each of these acts has an intentional goal.

I've been running my own business now for over 20 years, and there have been times when I have felt pulled in multiple directions. With every day busy, it can be tough to know if you are taking the right approach to reaching your goals.

I've worked with several business coaches during my years in business, all of whom have been instrumental in some aspect of my personal and professional development. Some have helped me to see my blind spots, some have helped to unlock my self-imposed limits.

Very early in my career as owner of my styling business, during a coaching session one of my coaches said to me, **"You can't steer a parked car."** I was having difficulty deciding which way to take my business. It seemed like every decision was too hard to implement. I had, in essence stalled, lost my momentum. His analogy was you have to keep moving forward. It's like sitting in your parked car. It will not move and you can't steer it. Start to change your life by taking one small step in one direction, then one more and one more. You will then slowly notice the change AND if you don't like that road you can turn right or left at a fork or even make a U-turn, but whichever way you go, you have started to build on that momentum.

No matter your circumstances whatever you choose to act upon, you can always adjust later. Like me, business goals can and will change over time. So, stop overthinking and get on with it. People are more likely to connect with and support businesses that align with their values and beliefs, so make sure you share yours with the world.

"I want to be in Vogue Magazine"

Meet Winifred Mills-Amu (Winnie), one of my clients, and a perfect example of how to follow the process. Winnie approached me back in 2020, the height of the Covid-19 pandemic. In her early 50s, working full-time as a Manager in Risk and Control in the banking sector in the United Arab Emirates and as a very busy mum, her goal was to launch a fashion label "Winnifred Mills" drawing on her Ghanaian heritage. I can recall vividly the first time I met her.

Bright, bubbly, and passionate about her vision for herself, Winnie's enthusiasm was infectious. She knew with absolute crystal clarity what she wanted to achieve; she just wasn't sure how to articulate her personal brand strategy to get ready to launch to the world. Winnie had big goals – she wanted her own fashion label, offering women designs that would fit and flatter, offering a strong silhouette. Winne also wanted to feature in **Vogue** magazine. With no existing social media platform and following, she was not at all daunted. Not even a pandemic could keep Winnie contained.

First and foremost, we got clear on what message Winnie wanted to share and put a plan in place to create content around her start-up journey. Her credible and personal story attracted local media opportunities, and even before her collection reached the market, her personal brand website was up and running, sharing with her followers and those new to her designs a behind-the-scenes journey. She was building her community presence.

Within 18 months, Winnie not only launched her fashion label, but she also got her feature in **Vogue** magazine. She added **Vanity Fair** to her treasure chest of goals achieved and most recently was included among the 12 inspirational and entrepreneurial women in the UAE and Africa networking group. Winnie has truly paved the way as a trailblazer and inspiration to others who are seeking to achieve their dreams.

What is the value of your personal brand?

Your personal brand audit may have revealed that you are missing values that matter to your sense of purpose. Those values may not have been entirely obvious at the outset, nonetheless they will set your direction.

Your personal brand values will act as your North Star and assist you to evaluate the content you write, posts you share and the way you engage with people. Whether that's a future employer or someone wanting to buy a product or service from you, connecting meaningfully with your audience requires authentic brand values.

What makes for a winning personal brand? Your personal brand is about WHO you are rather than about WHAT you do.

What are your core values and personal brand attributes?

Choosing three to five core values is an essential step in shaping your personal brand. These values serve as the guiding principles that underpin your character, behaviour and decisions. When your personal brand aligns with your chosen values, it communicates authenticity and integrity to those around you. It helps you build trust, connect with like-minded individuals and differentiates yourself in a crowded world. It also helps keep you on track with your social media strategy, and living in harmony with your values empowers you to make choices that are true to yourself and your vision, creating a more meaningful and purpose-driven personal brand that resonates with others.

When you choose your values, make sure you can clearly describe how your personal brand upholds each of them.

Here are a couple of examples from some of my clients:

Pilates teacher:
Warmth, education/knowledge, empowerment, compassion, mindfulness.

Business coach:
Integrity, results driven, simplicity, energy.

Event planner:
Creative, detail-oriented, reliability, professionalism.

Remember, goals can (and do) change

One of my clients who I worked with a few years ago is a perfect example of how goals change. At the outset she was clear with her goal setting; she wanted to become an executive coach working with large-scale organisations. She started coaching, but it wasn't long before she realised this wasn't aligned with what she truly wanted to do.

She made the decision to get even clearer on her goals. As is often the case, when you get down to the nitty gritty of defining goals, you realise there is another path to tread. This was indeed the case for my client. Whilst she was passionate about coaching, by reassessing her values she realised the area in which she wanted to coach was centred around sustainability. She had a desire to help businesses and people to, in her words, "become a force for good".

With a lot of hard work, she pivoted her offering and within six months had rebranded herself as a consultant and coach focusing on sustainability and climate action. She's on a mission to create a community of change-makers who can contribute actively to transforming the business world. To achieve this, she had to upskill her knowledge and reengineer her business model to reflect her sustainability-focused goal. Quite a shift and quite specific, but it has paid off. She has built a successful business around her passion. That is the power behind defined goal setting.

Enjoy the journey. It can take time to achieve your goals, they will rarely happen overnight. Whilst setting goals is important, it's also important that you embrace the experiences along the way. Try not to be too focused on a singular path, for as I have said goals can change over time, sometimes planned and sometimes unexpectedly. That's OK!

"A GOAL WRITTEN BECOMES INTENT, IT IS NO LONGER HOPES AND DREAMS."

In 2015, Dr Gail Matthews, a psychology professor at the Dominican University in California embarked on a study about goal setting. She found that "when people wrote down their goals, they were on average 33 per cent more successful in achieving them, than those who formulated outcomes in their heads."[5]

The reason? The act of choosing to write down your goals ignites an entirely new dimension of consciousness, because ideas and productivity reach the powerhouse that is your subconscious mind. By opening your subconscious mind, it enables you to SEE opportunities. We can all be great procrastinators – when you're too busy THINKING about your goals, you get tied up and never achieve them.

As a personal brand strategist, when I start working with my clients on goal setting, I ask them, "What's the first thing that comes to mind, and in no particular order?" Responses, I have found, can be either professional or personal. They often include everything from improving social media consistency or time management, to learning

---

[5] Roberts, K. (2023) 'The Power of Writing Down Your Goals: Evidence from Multiple Studies,' *theOAKJournal* [Preprint]. https://oakjournal.com/blogs/resources/the-power-of-writing-down-your-goals-evidence-from-multiple-studies.

new skills, or taking better care of physical and mental wellbeing. Getting clear on your goals is just the first step; in my experience the magic happens when you share your goals with others.

I met Natassia D'Souza, in 2020. Living in Dubai, Natassia was at the time working for a world-leading cosmetic brand. She had embarked upon an extensive personal journey, which was twofold; a weight loss program which saw her lose 65 kg and the launch of a new career as an emotional eating and weight-loss coach.

Natassia had found me through my social media channels. She saw that I had set an intention on my Instagram to run a half marathon. Now here's where I confess to you that I don't like running, never have done, so why would I even consider signing myself up for a challenge like this? As part of my desire to get in better shape, I wanted to test myself.

Like me, it transpired that Natassia did not enjoy running, but equally wanted to try out a new experience and test herself following her life-changing weight loss. We both had a common goal; we became, by default, accountable to each other to complete our goal.

From this single act of intent, Natassia's initial goal set about a series of events that has been instrumental in changing her life and her business model with astonishing results. What started out as training for a marathon went on to Natassia becoming one of my personal brand clients. She not only smashed her marathon training, but she also ran her first half marathon in a time of three hours and seven minutes, having only undertaken eight weeks of training. Goal setting to reality. That said, neither of us has actively run again, nor will we!

Step forward 12 months and with clear goal setting Natassia has elevated her style and incorporated new and innovative content into her growing social media platform. Her goal to elevate her style generated a fresh idea for us both. Remember what I said about opening your subconscious mind? We saw an opportunity to work together through Instagram, curating what has been some of mine and her most popular content using the hashtag: #KXNStyleNotSize.

The concept of #KXNStyleNotSize was to showcase clothing from high-street and designer stores and boutiques in differing sizes. I am short, 5'2", whilst Natassia is considered tall at 5'11", so we looked to showcase what a UK size 8 and 16 would look like worn on different frames.

Not only did we have so much fun creating the content, Natassia also picked up style tips that suited her enhanced personal brand and her new career as businesswomen and entrepreneur. She has directly monetised her personal brand with an additional revenue stream. It has generated a wardrobe full of new clothes, gifted by brands who were keen for her and me to showcase the looks through our social media channels.

Among her other documented goals that we set out were to deliver a personal branded website, organise a professional photoshoot, update her media profile pictures, and create media and speaking opportunities.

Where You Need to Go

All these actionable goals have had a compound effect on establishing a credible and authentic personal brand. Her consistent investment has resulted in a huge growth in her personal brand equity and increase in her "long-term savings account". Her bottom line has increased by 324 per cent in the 12 months since she began her personal brand journey with myself and Brand YOU Creators. Her value has increased exponentially, as has her self-belief in what she is doing not only for herself, but also for her burgeoning business.

Quite effortlessly, Natassia has deseeded the lemon and elevated her personal brand one pip at a time.

TOP TIP: SET GOALS AND REGULARLY REVIEW THEM

Start with things you have wanted to do, but haven't gotten around to doing, it all relates to the betterment of your personal brand. I like to think of it as experience over ego. It's often the little things that lead to the bigger things. Experience can bring richness in the content you can share with others.

Ask yourself the following four questions:

- What skills do I want to learn?
- Who do I want to help?
- What do I want to experience personally and professionally?
- Where do I want to visit?

> These may seem like statements, but they are in fact goals. You are, however, at this point setting goals, but giving yourself no clear timeline in which to achieve your goals. Some goals may, by design, happen sooner, some by default may span a greater period. You should never limit yourself or be constrained by what others think or feel or what society says is "acceptable".
>
> Once every six months, or at least every year, depending on what you have set as your intent, review your goals. In their entirety, your list of goals can look overwhelming, and it can seem like a very high mountain to climb.
>
> The trick is to break the list into sizable chapters to fit your life. Pick what is manageable instead of tackling the entire list. Some things may require more planning or require you to step way outside your comfort zone, running being a case in point for me. Yes, for sure it can seem scary. But think of the end game and what you could achieve when you set out to deseed the lemon.

I took an excerpt out of my 2017 goal list to share the exact process. I asked myself the same four questions.

1. What skills did I want to learn?

MY GOAL:

To learn how to cook four signature dishes each year.

I'm no foodie, nor was I particularly interested in cooking until I hit my mid 30s, when I met my now husband, who is a die-hard foodie. It was a big-ticket win successfully achieved. I am still committing to this goal each year and am getting better and better. For someone who could not cook at all, my pièce de résistance is a tasty Beef Wellington. It's a learnable skill.

2. Who did I want to help?

MY GOAL:

To work with a minimum of 30 clients within the year.

I signed up and mentored those desired 30 clients!

3. What was a professional or personal experience I would like to do?

MY GOAL:

A date with Tony Robbins.

I signed up and completed "A Date with Destiny" in 2018!

4. Where would I like to visit?

MY GOAL:

To go to Nairobi and have afternoon tea with the giraffes.

Like many former cabin crew our love to travel lives on long after our career, and I still have a bucket list of where I would like to visit, which fortunately is very similar to my mum's. In 2017, we set off to East Africa, and stayed at Giraffe Manor to have an iconic afternoon tea with the giraffes.

These goals were not achieved in one year, they spanned a period of four years, especially the cooking one. Details play a big part in achieving your goals – it's all about focusing on deseeding the lemon. Once you gain clarity on the bigger goals, they very often result in much smaller goals being achieved more easily.

For example, you may be a business owner who, during your Google search and audit, found only three pictures of yourself online, zero video content and an outdated LinkedIn page. You might set your bigger goals to:

- Improve your online credibility.
- Share content and opinions more consistently.
- Grow your LinkedIn following to over 2,500 connections.

Smaller goals will look something like this:

- Get new pictures taken which will give you content to share.
- Identify three to five content pillars (more of this when we get to Slice Four) to discuss on social media.
- Update your LinkedIn bio and share content twice a week.
- Write a monthly blog.

To make it ever more actionable, take these goals, and break them down further into daily goals. These could include:

- Book a photoshoot.
- Choose three to four outfits for the shoot.
- Write a post based on one of your content pillars (don't worry, I explain content pillars in detail in Chapter 10).
- Schedule time to write a blog for your website.
- Connect with five new people on LinkedIn.

Breaking your goals down into smaller, more manageable steps is vital – this is what will help you achieve them. One of the main reasons people stall when it comes to achieving their goals is because they focus too much on the perceived barriers rather than looking at the steps, no matter how small, that they **can** take.

So, once you've set those big goals, work backwards and dissect them to break them into much smaller, very manageable tasks. This will not only help you actually achieve your goals, but is also a great way to ensure you're setting realistic time frames. Once you've mapped out all the steps ahead, you can estimate how long you need to complete each one, and what other resources you might require, such as money.

Remember: the key to achieve successful outcomes is to work backwards. Figure out when you want to achieve something to see if the outcome is realistic.

Create your desire statement

Another strategy that has really helped me and countless clients, friends and those I mentor make progress towards achieving our goals is creating a desire statement; a declaration statement about what you intend to do.

I've always looked to develop my own personal and professional skills by working with business coaches. One such coach shared with me the benefits of embarking on this specific exercise, writing a desire statement.

For years I was a vision board addict! Every year, my carefully created collages of images and words represented my wishes and goals, they were intended to inspire and motivate me. Whilst some of my visions were achieved, others were not.

Take the example of my goal for Tony Robbins' "Date with Destiny", which sat at the bottom right-hand corner of my vision board. Each New Year's Day, I created a new vision board, and guess what? My "Date with Destiny" was still sitting waiting to happen.

I decided to embrace the concept of writing a desire statement. Time to make my "Date with Destiny" happen. As I thoughtfully created my desire statement, I was able to focus my attention and harness my energy to achieve my desire. Rather than focusing on the perceived barriers, which in this case was primarily the cost, I instead broke my goal down. Working backwards from the goal in mind, breaking down the stages of what it would take to get to "it", everything became manageable. It was a game changer.

At the time, I hadn't fully embraced the belief that the subconscious mind does not know what is real and not real, or if an event has happened. So, if you say something has happened, you can get your subconscious mind to believe that it has, even if it has not yet occurred.

Applying the principles from my then business coach, that "it" became possible. I no longer have a vision board, because adopting the concept of writing a desire statement has led to even greater results, goal selection and the delivery of a TEDx talk.

Karen Osman, a British novelist, writing coach and previous client of mine, wrote a desire statement back in 2018. She then misplaced it. Some eight months later, Karen happened to come across it, reread it and immediately called me.

What Karen had written down when we worked together had, she said, "just become a reality." In her desire statement, she had documented that she would become a published author and land a three-book deal. Not just a one-book deal, she was looking for three! Eight months later, that's exactly what happened. "It's incredible," she said.

An extract from my desire statement written in 2018 reads like this:

> *I TRAVELLED TO EAST AFRICA WITH MY MUM, IT WAS HER 60TH YEAR. WE ARRIVED IN NAIROBI AND STAYED IN THE NATIONAL PARK WHERE WE STAYED AT AN ECOLODGE ON THE EDGE OF THE AFRICAN GRASSLANDS.*
>
> *MORNINGS WERE SPENT ON THE MOST INCREDIBLE GAME DRIVES, WE SAW MAJESTIC ANIMALS IN THE WILD, LIONS, ZEBRAS, WHITE RHINOS AND GIRAFFES. WE SPENT TWO NIGHTS AT GIRAFFE MANOR, WHERE WE WINED AND DINED, AND HAD AFTERNOON TEA WITH THE GIRAFFES – A HOT WATER AND LEMON IN A FINE BONE CHINA CUP FOR ME. IT WAS AN INCREDIBLE EXPERIENCE; IT WAS MORE THAN ANYTHING I EVER EXPECTED.*

I achieved everything I had detailed in my desire statement above, and then some.

Can you imagine what it would be like if, say, a year into the future, you bump into someone you haven't seen in a while. I would imagine my conversation would go a bit like this.

"Hi Kelly, how are you, I haven't seen you in a long while, what's been happening?"

I would be able to respond with absolute clarity, thanks to my desire statement: "Hi, yes, it's been a while, I've had an amazing year. My business has grown by 75 per cent. I launched my podcast which has featured more than 20 incredible interviews with entrepreneurs from all over the world. I've signed to work with 30 new clients, and I went on a Date with Destiny with the one and only Tony Robbins! It's been an incredible ride."

How would your desire statement read? How would it look if you were seeking a promotion, how would it feel, where are you sitting, what are you doing? Perhaps you are preparing your talk for TEDx – what does it feel like, where are you standing, who is sitting in front of you?

TOP TIP: WRITE YOUR DESIRE STATEMENT

Here's a structure to get you started; write yours with positive descriptors. Use words that describe what it feels and looks like, where you are and what you are doing.

It's December 25th. The year is _____
This has been the best _____ months/year ever.

I have achieved _____

I completed _____
as part of my personal brand strategy.

I met _____

I travelled to _____

I experienced _____

I felt _____

Keep your desire statement current, if you find that you no longer actively read it or it no longer resonates, compose a new one. You can do this as many times in a year as feels right for you.

Setting personal brand goals is an essential step in building a strong and authentic personal brand. Identifying your core values, as discussed earlier, and then identifying your strengths, and unique qualities, are the secret sauce. As your personal brand is essentially a reflection of who you are, an understanding of your strengths and uniqueness sets you apart and enables you to leverage what makes you special.

So, how do you identify what makes you special? Begin by considering your professional experiences, accomplishments and personal characteristics. What are you exceptionally good at? What skills or talents have garnered you recognition or praise? These are often your strengths. Additionally, think about what makes you stand out from others in your field. Your unique qualities could be a blend of your experiences, passions and the way you approach challenges.

Gathering feedback from peers, mentors and clients, which is what we do with our clients who really want to dive deeper into their personal brand, means you can develop a clear and compelling personal brand that resonates with your audience.

KEY PIP TAKEAWAYS

IDENTIFY UP TO FIVE PERSONAL BRAND VALUES.

CLEARLY DEFINE YOUR GOALS, BREAK THEM DOWN INTO SMALLER GOALS AND USE THESE TO HELP INFORM YOUR PERSONAL BRAND STRATEGY.

WRITE A PERSONAL BRANDING DESIRE STATEMENT BASED ON YOUR GOALS AS IF THEY HAVE ALREADY HAPPENED.

Chapter 4:

PITCH TO PROFIT

In today's fast-paced and competitive business world, the ability to make your personal brand stand out and make a lasting first impression is paramount. Yet the one aspect that is often the hardest for most to convey is a well-rehearsed elevator pitch, that equally doesn't sound so rehearsed that ChatGPT wrote it for you.

The pitch that says… who are you, who do you help?

An elevator pitch is a concise, compelling summary of your product, service, your job role or even an idea that can be delivered in the span of an elevator ride. We all know our attention spans have become shorter, so your elevator pitch is an opportunity to grab someone's attention quickly and make them want to learn more.

To make your elevator pitch great, as a general rule, aim to keep it to around 30 seconds or less. However, elevator pitches can vary in length depending on your industry and the message you're pitching. But more on that later!

Just remember you are not travelling in an elevator that's going up 127 floors in the Burj Khalifa, aka the world's tallest building. Nobody likes a waffler.

An elevator pitch is a brief, but incredibly powerful interaction, provided you have honed your personal brand to make the right first impression. Delivering your pitch well is an essential skill. It will, if you have taken the time to deseed the lemon, open doors to opportunities and propel your visibility and credibility.

"SIMPLE THINGS ARE ALWAYS THE MOST DIFFICULT."

– Carl Jung

Why then do so many people find creating and delivering their elevator pitch so challenging?

As an entrepreneur or business owner (established or emerging), you may have a great many ideas and, therefore, struggle to articulate your messaging. Imposter syndrome or a lack of clarity can make it tough to distil your message into a conscious and impactful format.

It may be that you cannot see the whole situation because you're looking too closely at the smaller details, and that's clouding your ability to identify the essence of what you are offering and just how to articulate it clearly. As the old saying goes, "You can't see the wood for the trees."

I certainly understand where you're coming from if this is how you're feeling as you're reading this book, having fallen into that trap myself many years ago. In my very early days of personal styling, I wore many hats. Not only was I styling individual clients, I was also doing photoshoots for magazine publications, and interior styling which was targeted at the growing expat community arriving in the city. I also embarked on establishing an online gift registry, which I quickly sold!

There is definitely value in versatility and being well-rounded, but I had spread myself way too thin. Not only did I confuse myself as to what I was trying to do, but I confused my clients. This was way before the days of defining my personal brand, and I was struggling.

I had just started to work with my first-ever coach. I recall quite vividly his words to me, "You don't want to be a Jack of all trades and master of none, get clear on who your client is, what you love doing and focus on that." Once that message had crystallised it was full steam ahead. I refined my elevator pitch goal, dropped the extra services, and focused.

It served as an excellent piece of advice and is a process that is embedded in my clients' personal brand strategies having experienced the value of it first-hand.

The value of clarity

A few years ago, I was approached by Leanne Foy who was struggling to identify what her new elevator pitch was now she had started her business. You may be reading this book and feel that this resonates with where you are in life at this moment. She felt unable to express who she was and what she was doing; unable to articulate her direction and purpose.

She approached me to ask for a one-off session to focus specifically on her message and elevator pitch. Whilst this is something I offer my clients; it was not normally an approach I took as a sole project. I did, however, agree. I could see there was something that I could offer her that could make the change for her. So often it can be easier for a third party to **"see the wood from the trees."**

As an outsider, I was not involved in her day-to-day details, and I was also not emotionally involved, but that didn't mean that I could not be invested in helping her to step outside self-imposed barriers. I understood her generic principles. As a dispassionate outsider my experience was able to direct her to what improvements she needed to make. In her case it was quite simple; she was lacking a refined elevator pitch.

To create a polished elevator pitch you need to think about who you are, what your mission is, what your value proposition is and who your target audience is. In doing so, you will gain a deeper understanding of your business, resulting in the ability to communicate your messaging with greater confidence and conviction.

She nailed it in just 30 minutes. Such was the success of our bespoke session she signed up and became one of my Brand YOU Creators clients. Leanne's pitch is now: "**I help SMEs grow their network, visibility and revenue through creating strategic growth plans, events and professional development programs.**"

Weaving your elevator pitch naturally into conversation becomes an art. The more you practise it the better you will become, and the greater the rewards you will see. If you can sum up the value you offer in a succinct and compelling way it paves the way for your professional successes. That said, an elevator pitch isn't always an opportunity to close a deal, but a chance to capture attention and encourage a future conversation. You never know, it could become a factor in securing you that promotion you have dreamed of, a new contract or a meaningful connection that brings even greater success as you journey along the road.

It's also important that you don't limit yourself to just one elevator pitch. There will be situations when you need to focus on one aspect of what you do over another, so it pays to be prepared. Come up with three elevator pitches, each of which articulates what you do and how you can help in a slightly different way. It can help to imagine delivering your pitch to people in different industries – what might someone in finance want to know versus someone in PR for example? Tailor your pitch accordingly.

I had my lightbulb moment when I was visiting London back in 2014. I had been nominated for an award – Communicator of the Year at the Scottish Fashion Awards. The ceremony was being held at Somerset House. I was there on my own, no plus ones were invited and I confess I did feel a little outside my comfort zone.

Standing alone, the organiser who I knew approached me, and said she would like to introduce me to her friend who worked in Human Resources (HR). I quickly thought which one of my pitches would be most relevant and interesting to the organiser's friend.

I shared with her clearly what I did and knowing she worked in HR, added in a little more depth around my experiences as a speaker working with many organisations to empower employees to dress with purpose in the workplace, as this was more relevant.

It later transpired that the person I was speaking to was Head of HR at Arsenal Football Club. Arriving back in Dubai she emailed me, enquiring about booking me as a speaker to present a keynote about personal brand, public presentation and style to all their VIP Hosts and Hostesses at their annual training day later that year. It was a substantial dollar contract, and has become a poignant story to highlight the power of a great elevator pitch that I share with clients.

This particular elevator pitch went something like this:

"Hi, I'm Kelly, a celebrity stylist (we were, after all, at a star-studded awards ceremony). I work with organisations, CEOs and their employees, educating them about how their personal style and image impacts all they do, personally and professionally. I empower them to dress for success, with confidence, and in doing so enable them to project a stronger public image."

An elevator pitch provides you with a framework for storytelling. In my experience, humans are wired to respond to narratives, and by intertwining a compelling story into your pitch you captivate your audience on an emotional level. Stories have the power to inspire, connect and leave a lasting impression of your personal brand.

Where to use an elevator pitch for your personal brand

Beyond its application in chance encounters in elevators, your pitch can be utilised in a variety of settings. Whether you're attending networking events, industry conferences, or even social gatherings, having a well-crafted pitch that effortlessly drips off your tongue ensures that you're always prepared to seize opportunities. It's your perfect opportunity to deseed the lemon, because it's a chance to engage with potential clients, make them remember you and perhaps even refer someone else to you if they don't require what you do.

My first-ever paid client came via a friend who I played hockey with. When I spoke to him it sparked his interest, prompted curiosity and led to a business opportunity. By capturing the attention and interest of your audience, you create a foundation for building relationships and exploring potential partnerships or collaborations.

Your elevator pitch can help you succinctly highlight your skills, experience, and unique qualities that make you a strong candidate when attending an interview for a new job. How many times have you been asked to tell someone something about yourself? Imagine if you had a ready to roll elevator pitch.

Or your elevator pitch can serve as a concise introduction to your product or service, highlighting its benefits and addressing the client's pain points and why what you do is the solution. It's an opportunity to sell yourself, and your personal brand. You may hate to sell, but sales calls and meetings all have the potential to reach new clients and secure new business for you.

Have you ever watched an episode of the TV shows **Dragons' Den** or **Shark Tank**? Entrepreneurs look to present a compelling and concise overview of their business ideas to investors or judges. They are a great forum, but how many times have you seen someone with a great product or service not make the mark, when perhaps their elevator pitch was not quite as articulate as the Dragons had hoped?

Take one great example: former Portsmouth taxi driver Rachel Lowe, from series one of **Dragons' Den**. She was looking for £75,000 in investment in return for a 30 per cent equity stake in a new board game called **Destination London,** a board game inspired by London's city streets. Entrepreneur Lowe's investment pitch was rejected. One of the "dragons" Rachel Elnaugh said, "It doesn't seem like you've prepared very well to come in front of us today." The dragons felt that Lowe couldn't have a basic business discussion about her target market.

However, her elevator pitch did hit the mark elsewhere. Lowe went on to secure alternative funding to produce **Destination London**. In 2008 her game was a top seller, knocking some of our best known games off the shelves, like the well-established **Monopoly**. She has even bagged an MBE!

Another such story comes from Brewdog, which appeals to my Scottish roots. Homebrew enthusiasts James Watt and Martin Dickie started a home brew venture from their garage in Aberdeenshire. They went to the dragons looking for a £100,000 investment in return for 20 per cent of their business. They were rejected by the producers on the basis that, **"their business was not deemed to be novel enough or with enough growth potential".**

Having been valued at £2 billion by Forbes in 2020 it would have been one of the most lucrative investments in **Dragons' Den** history, had any of them invested.[6]

---

6   *Yahoo is part of the Yahoo family of brands* (2023), 2 October, available at: https://uk.news.yahoo.com/made-chelsea-star-georgia-toffolo-135538327.html.

Articulating your elevator pitch

If you are looking to be seen, one such place where you can find an audience for your elevator pitch is online platforms and social media, such as LinkedIn or X. These forums allow you to showcase your pitch, albeit using limited characters, to convey your professional value. Despite the limited character or word count, these platforms can serve as a powerful introduction to attract attention and encourage further engagement.

Your elevator pitch must be concise and should always provoke interest that will allow follow-on questions. It's all about engagement – you need to position yourself in the mind of any potential investor, you need to be able to clearly define what you do and your key product or service and define your USP (unique selling point)!

TOP TIP: FORMULATE YOUR ELEVATOR PITCH

Think!
- What is your niche?
- What is the current situation?
- What is the desired situation?
- Keep your pitch brief.
  Define your message in a simple sentence.

I use this simple equation with all my clients to get them to focus on the simplicity of an elevator pitch:

I help _____ to get _____
by _____

One business coach recently told me that they didn't like the use of the word "help" in my elevator pitch equation, because they didn't feel it worked in a coaching context. So, for clarity, the equation I've shared is designed to be a simple framework from which to structure your elevator pitch. You don't have to stick to my wording for your finished pitch – in fact, I'd encourage you not to and to find your own.

However, starting with the basic idea of who you help (or support, or work with – whatever terminology floats your boat), what you help them do/achieve and how you do that means you cover all of the key elements of a great elevator pitch.

Everything you actively do to validate your personal brand is to differentiate yourself from competitors. A compelling elevator pitch communicates not only what you do, but also why you do it and what sets you apart. It conveys your passion, expertise and the value you bring to the table, making it easier for potential clients or partners to choose you over the competition.

The power of the elevator pitch

Christiana and I first met at the start of the summer of 2021 in a little café in Dubai. A dynamic New York go-getter, she confessed that she was looking for help with her personal brand style which she needed to enhance for her upcoming appearances on a local TV show. Her approach to me was because of my past life in the personal styling space. As we chatted, it became evident, quite quickly, that Christiana had bigger aspirations. Fuelled also by the pandemic, Christiana had identified a gap in the Dubai dating market. She had embarked on a study path to become an accredited dating coach and wanted to go one step further with a business idea.

As with many of my clients, small ideas become even larger, and Christiana was no exception. It was clear at that point that I could help her way beyond personal style, we were on a whole new level with her personal brand messaging.

Signing on with Brand YOU Creators, we worked to define the strategy required to launch her business concept. It began with articulating her elevator pitch. Putting pen to paper, Christiana crafted and refined her elevator pitch. It enabled her to cement some really BIG personal brand goals. Her messaging was pitch perfect:

> Christiana Maxion, better known as The Dubai Matchmaker, is solving dating in Dubai by offering unlimited matchmaking opportunities for high-net-worth and ultra-high-net-worth men with the globe's largest matchmaking database and a success rate of 96 per cent.

At Brand YOU Creators we designed Christiana's logo, website and branding guidelines. From that first meeting in that Dubai café Christiana's tireless, but focused, pursuit saw her launch The Dubai Matchmaker, where today she successfully helps United Arab Emirates-based men and women find their ideal partner through well-thought-out and professionally executed matchmaking.

Christiana has since been featured in over 200 global publications, undertaken countless radio interviews, launched a podcast and quit her full-time job to follow her dream. She has also 10x her personal brand income. Christiana's acceptance of accountability has undoubtedly led to her success as The Dubai Matchmaker. She continues to invest in her brand equity, with her sights firmly set on expanding across the United Arab Emirates as the premier matchmaker in the region. As I write this, she is even about to launch her own app: MAXION.

Having clear personal brand goals will help you to stay motivated and focused. You can track your progress, celebrate your successes and adjust your strategy as needed to stay on track. Don't lose sight of the investment you make when creating your personal brand strategy, from auditing your personal brand to getting clear on your goals, clarity in your message and values. Each element will set you apart from competition and have you showing up as the best possible version of you. Deseed the lemon.

KEY PIP TAKEAWAYS

IF SOMEONE ASKS WHAT YOU DO, BE PREPARED TO STREAMLINE WHAT YOU SAY YOU DO, FOCUS ON THE ESSENTIALS.

KEEP YOUR ELEVATOR PITCH SHORT AND SWEET — THINK OF IT AS A SALES PITCH.

PRACTICE, PRACTICE, PRACTICE.

SLICE TWO:

STYLE

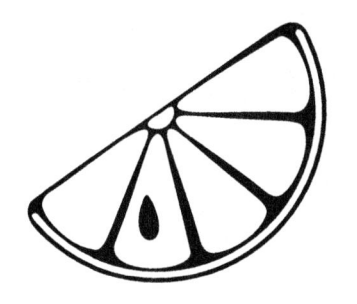

Your style is so much more than what you wear, it's how you express yourself to the world. Consider the persona you want to present; use your clothes and style to build a memorable personal brand. Your style will reflect what you stand for and who you are, and serve to create an outstanding first impression, when done well!

As a child I always loved expressing myself through my style. Fashion has always been a way of expressing myself – as you can see from my earlier story of my somewhat colourful hairstyles. My love of fashion goes way back to the early days when I would immerse myself in the annual arrival, just after Christmas, of the hardbound clothing catalogues that my mum subscribed to – Grattan, Littlewoods, Kays. Who can remember those days?

Long before the internet, I would sit patiently, eagerly waiting for the post to arrive, the frosty window panes steamed clean with my hot breath of anticipation. I couldn't wait to be transported into the pages to see what was hot for the new season. Pouring over those glossy, jam-packed pages, I would spend hours dreaming of what I could buy. Unfortunately, an eight-year-old's pocket money could never quite stretch far enough. My imagination could though.

In the '90s, my passion for fashion landed me a job in the high-street fashion retailer Next. Subconsciously, I think I had always wanted to become a stylist. That was long before I realised that it could be a lucrative profession, outside the remit of a store, and one that you could get paid (very well) for.

You could always find me hovering around the fitting room. It was here where I found my feet, spending my time helping customers, making suggestions on how they might look to enhance their style, sorting out sizes and completing a look with accessories.

Enthusiastically I would make sure every customer had an amazing experience. It was a constant surprise to see the lack of confidence customers had when it came to what to wear and what suited them. It put a whole new spin around the mindset of "does my bottom look big in this?"

Desperately wanting to reinforce their confidence and boost their self-esteem, I found that just by taking time talking to customers (something that my school report card indicated I outclassed myself in) I found it easy to put them at ease and help them to explore their style. Inadvertently, I had found my creative niche. It was gratifying to be able to help people to connect with their style and for them to gain an insight into what could be their personal brand. As I excelled in every interaction with my customers, I set out to deseed the lemon.

What's your style?

Style is an indisputable and intrinsic part of your personal brand. There is a ripple effect in everything you do. If you are unhappy with your style, it will reflect in your personal brand. You will not enjoy having your photograph taken, which means you have less content to post and are, therefore, potentially less visible. People relate to people, over the faceless logo of a person or their company.

One of my most rewarding styling experiences was with a six-year-old girl. Yes, you can style anyone at any age; everyone has their own unique reason for coming to me. Her mum was one of my retainer clients. She mentioned that her daughter had been going through a very tough period in her life, and her self-esteem needed a bit of boosting.

I had met her daughter on several occasions, and nothing seemed evident to me. My client explained that her daughter had had cleft palate reconstructive surgery at birth, which was incredibly successful, yet some children at school were still giving her a really hard time. Being unkind is not just the domain of children, in all walks of life one or another of us will have experienced some kind of calling out because of a difference, children, however, can be horrors!

My brief was to go shopping and find outfits that her mum would not normally pick and arrange to have a professional photoshoot at the end of our styling session. The power of style!

As our session concluded and we arrived for her photoshoot, that little girl was beaming beautifully with her experience. Confidence buoyed, she told me that she felt like a princess and in truth she looked just like one too. My memories of that little six-year-old, staring with delight at her reflection in the mirror, decked out in a funky, yet feminine Zara kids' ensemble, remains a picture-perfect moment for us both.

Slice Two: Style

You too can have that picture-perfect moment when you stand in front of the mirror. Own your personal brand; establish your style personality, evaluate your communication style, and prepare yourself for your next photoshoot. If you can understand the nuances of how to deseed the lemon with your style, creating your personal brand will confirm you as the expert in your field.

Chapter 5:

WHY STYLE MATTERS

When I was a celebrity stylist, regardless of whether a male or female engaged me to work with them, I was fascinated when I checked inside their closet. Navigating through the contents, you had no idea what you would find. What I could almost always guarantee though was that in our session we would often unearth a suit of some description. When asked when it was last worn the reply was invariably, "I only ever bring it out to wear for an interview or my first week of a new job." Why is it you only make an effort to get the job, not afterwards?

What you wear to work is a direct representation of who you are and it reflects how you conduct yourself in business. How you dress matters. Making the effort to show up as the best version of yourself is all about how you deseed the lemon. Remember what my granny said about a few rogue pips spoiling her perfect cup of hot water with lemon.

Dress the part

Many people in business choose to simplify their style to represent their personal brand, it's called a signature style. Not to be confused with a style uniform – you may have read that Steve Jobs wore the same outfit day in, day out, sporting what became his trademark black turtleneck and plain slacks. Mark Zuckerberg adopts a simple statement grey T-shirt. There's a difference between a signature style and a uniform, namely that a signature style is about consistency, not repetition. A style uniform will stand out day to day and stick to both specific colours and specific styles you've chosen for each item. A signature style will have some aspects that remain the same – such as a bold accessory, but not the same one, colour palette or silhouette – while other aspects will change from day to day.

I present my **Deseed the Lemon** keynote to large corporate clients and global luxury hospitality groups. They seek me out because they have a similar internal issue; employees who show up to work dressed inconsistently and failing to meet professional company brand values. They fail to demonstrate a plausible personal brand. These organisations all seek a common goal, to deseed the lemon.

Why is it then that individuals in pursuit of defining their personal brand miss the mark? Whilst style matters, an extensive budget to purchase appropriate attire is not required. I have, over my years in personal branding, successfully styled clients with tiny budgets (and big ideas). They have gone on to achieve some of the biggest wins with their personal brand style.

Over the years, I've lost count of the number of times I have heard, "I don't have time," when I've asked why someone's style isn't a priority for them. Planning is the key when it comes to what to wear and when. Every Sunday, I take the time to organise my closet and plan my outfits for the week, whether it's working from home, attending the office, networking, events or a business trip. Practice makes perfect. I am also not the only one – after watching the Beckham documentary on Netflix, it turns out he is also a big planner for his weekly wardrobe!

Look good, feel good

Self-reflection is always a good principle to apply when it comes to style. Often, we can get stuck in a rut of buying the clothes that often outgrow our brand. It's sensible to audit your style, brands change, body shape can alter and what worked for you from one year to the next may very well no longer work. That's where an expert can help you to take an objective view to keep current.

I worked for 10 years with a client, styling her entire closet for every day of the week. Her closet looks were styled not only for her work life, but for her personal life too. She never needed to think about what to wear or when. Her style evolved as she defined her personal brand. Today her brand remains as relevant as it did when we started, and she now has the tools to do this for herself.

That all-important feel-good factor is generated by what you are wearing. When you feel good in what you're wearing, you automatically project positivity and engage with greater confidence, creating the right first impression; a win-win situation.

Why is it, then, that so many of us (yes, even you) can understand the criticality of making an impactful first impression, then fail to sustain that momentum? The answer is a lack of consistency! How you style yourself reflects your personal brand and just as you need to be consistent with your personal branding activities, so too do you need to be consistent with your style.

Fashion faux pas often receive the most attention, and not the good kind. They are unwanted and will come with consequences. I was hired by a Dubai-based public relations communication company after they nearly lost a pitch to one of their biggest clients. That client will remain anonymous, other than they were a luxury car manufacturer.

Having handed this client to one of their top account executives, he attended the luxury car manufacturer to deliver his pitch wearing a suit; good start you would think. Eminently acceptable? Later that day the client called the PR company to say that as one of the world's leading manufacturers they delivered exceptional customer service experience to their clients; they were all about the details. They explained that the account executive had turned up looking sloppy – whilst he had presented in a suit, he had failed to tie his tie.

The lack of attention to detail by the account executive nearly cost the PR company that account all because that account executive did not meet the brand values of the luxury car manufacturer.

Deseed The Lemon

You don't become the best, especially in leading customer service roles, by making do with slap-dash standards. The account executive had, in fact, failed to deseed the lemon and the importance of how you dress and present yourself was lost on him.

Working for one of the world's leading, award-winning airlines, I quickly learned that grooming was one of their key priorities. It's one area where they have consistently received rewards, in addition to their exemplary safety standards.

I confess I often found their tight guidelines frustrating, especially when I was transitioning from crew and finding my feet in the outside world of fashion. Frequently I would strive to express my own style, only to be told to temper my style. If you have ever flown with Emirates, I was the girl with the short spiky hair, no matter what I tried it would never conform to a bun in those days. I can see though why their grooming guidelines work so well and why their awards are well deserved. It's all related to consistency.

I can never understand when a client tells me, "I don't care what I wear to work," or gestures to an item of clothing and says, "It's old, I just wear it to work." No matter where you work, whether you are required to wear a uniform or not, and if you are serious about developing your personal brand, your style must signal who you are.

Using style to find your tribe

I'm all about making sure that I spend time with people who are aligned with what I am looking for in my own life. "You're the average of the five people you spend the most time with." I've lost count of the times I have come across this saying attributed to Jim Rohn, a motivational speaker. I use it often myself in my keynotes.

For those of us in the workplace, it may surprise you to learn that if you are in full-time employment, you will spend at least a third of your life in the workplace. In my view that's way too much time to spend being untidy and badly dressed. If your office environment is quite sloppy and casual, chances are you will be dressing the same. Flip the coin and have dinner with friends who are fashion conscious, you are more likely to dress up and make more of an effort. Just because everyone else around you dresses in a sloppy and casual manner doesn't mean you have to. You can set standards and lead the pack. Either representing a company brand or your personal brand, deseed the lemon.

Still don't believe me? There is a science behind this. Clinical psychologist Dr Jennifer Baumgartner is the author of **You Are What You Wear, What Your Clothes Reveal About You.** She uses the phrase "psychology of dress". It's her view that psychology determines our clothing choices. How we choose to dress ourselves can help us overcome key psychological issues that we face in our everyday life and in our work.

What you are wearing will inadvertently have those around you make assumptions about your personal brand, whether about your job, your spending habits, your lifestyle or even your personality. It stands to reason, therefore, that clothes become our social and economic indicators. If you don't want people to misunderstand you, then you should consider what you're wearing and how you appear.

Don't get me wrong, we all have bad days, but don't make it a habit! If you want to avoid generating a less than positive impression, take the time to think about your style. I often use the following simple alternatives that people might be thinking about your personal brand style, regardless of how you perceive them:

Wet hair = "Slept in, don't really care"

Outdated clothing = "Outdated ideas"

Overstuffed wallets or handbags = "Distracted and messy, unorganised"

Bitten Nails = "Unhygienic, anxious personality"

Unpolished, scuffed shoes = "Doesn't pay attention to detail"

Too much make-up = "What are they hiding?"

Doesn't smile = "Can be mistaken for a bad attitude"

Why Style Matters

If you are wrestling with ideas on how to dress and style yourself, there is nothing wrong with asking for help. The clients I work with today see what to wear and how to style as an investment in their personal brand, a lifelong and life-changing commitment. I use my past experience as a stylist to emphasise to my clients that this matters for their personal brand strategy. What they wear is as important as choosing the logo, font size, writing and colours when considering their personal brand.

Stylists are no longer the domain of celebrities. We all need experts in their field, so why shouldn't you engage the services of a stylist? If your closet is not working for you, they can help you to define your style. You wouldn't cut your own hair – unless perhaps you're a precocious five-year-old who has gotten her hands on a pair of contraband scissors and gone to work on her blonde locks (the least said about this incident probably the better!). When your laptop breaks, you ask a technician to fix it. When your car isn't working, you take it to the garage.

According to research, it takes one-tenth of a second to form a first impression. Your appearance, body language and how you are dressed help people make an instant evaluation of you. What you wear is one part of the success equation. Nonverbal gestures, eye contact and smell all contribute to how you are measured, perceived, and judged.

"CLOTHES MEAN NOTHING UNTIL SOMEONE LIVES IN THEM."

– Marc Jacobs

One of my very first business meetings was with a young, vibrant, and very professional businesswomen. I think I would have been around 24, as it was quite soon after launching my styling agency.

Nicole turned up to present her product to me, a collection of leather bags and corporate accessories. My first impression was her sophisticated yet understated style, her whole attire was immaculate. She sat down beside me, opened her very elegant and organised leather handbag, pulled out an equally beautiful leather-bound notebook and located her Montblanc pen.

From head to toe she had left no detail unattended. My eyes were even drawn to her handbag contents, scrupulously organised. Nicole exemplified the term deseed the lemon and it was not just Nicole's attire – her tone, expression and body language were equally polished.

I consciously formed my opinion of her as an organised, meticulous and detail-oriented person who takes pride in her appearance, and thus, in her work. I credit Nicole with a great deal, she was a huge influence in how I developed my personal brand in my early business days.

Why Style Matters

Everyone does deserve to look and feel good. You may be a mum, running errands, dashing to pick up children from the school gates, presenting a new pitch to a potential investor or signing royalty. All eyes will be on you. What you wear can act as your armour of confidence.

I had a client a number of years ago book a personal styling session. She was about to come face to face with her ex-husband's new wife. It's probably safe to say meeting anyone's new partner or spouse for the first time is daunting regardless of ex marital history. My client was hosting a baby shower for her daughter.

Baby showers, if you have not been to one, can be a strange mix, ranging from dressed to the nines to super casual. My client was quite clear on her styling goal, something to give her confidence, that was stylish and that enabled her to feel comfortable whilst supporting her daughter hosting her event. With over 1,200 retail outlets in Dubai Mall alone, it was easy to accomplish her goal. A few weeks later I received a thank you card, with a photograph of her at the event. The baby shower and first meeting was a success and she felt great. Clothes do not only have a symbolic meaning, the physical experience of wearing them has a profound effect on how you show up as the best version of you.

When was the last time you bought something from the shops, or picked an outfit from your closet and it made you feel happy? It can be an instantaneous feeling for some, for others it may take a little longer. If you have ever found yourself in a style rut, you will know what I mean. You can feel it. Wearing the same clothes day in, day out; uninspired by your appearance. The magic of style happens when you have an open mind.

Your style, and creating a great first impression, isn't about making the biggest spend or owning the latest labels. Your closet reflects who you are and how the contents make you feel. It is important to realise that what's in your closet isn't a frivolous investment – discount of course the vast number of designer shoes that don't fit bought in the wrong size at a sample sale!

When I work with clients on their personal brand strategy, an integral part of their journey is a personal brand photoshoot. Embedded into your strategy should be the importance of quality, high-resolution and relevant photographs. You don't want photos to date too quickly, so styling for a photoshoot should reveal the authentic you and reflect who you are. More about what to prepare for a photoshoot in Chapter 9.

Personal style goes way beyond just clothing and grooming choice; it's a reflection of who you are, how you not only perceive yourself, but also how you wish to be perceived by the world. Through my lens of fashion and personal branding, it's evident that the way we dress holds intense power in shaping our interactions, opportunities and self confidence.

Whether you're stepping into a new business, job interview, meeting or simply going about your day, the clothes you wear send a message about your commitment, attention to detail and the value you place on your personal brand. The concept of deseeding the lemon reminds us that even

Why Style Matters

small oversights can have profound effects on how we're perceived, just as a few rogue pips can spoil the perfect cup of hot water with lemon. It's not just about appearing the part; it's about embodying it consistently.

Style is not a luxury, but an investment in the presentation of your best self.

KEY PIP TAKEAWAYS

EMBRACE YOUR PERSONAL STYLE AS A REFLECTION OF YOUR AUTHENTIC SELF:

Recognise that personal style is more than just clothing; it reflects your identity, self-perception and the image you want to project to the world. Understand that the way you present yourself through fashion holds significant influence over how you're perceived and the opportunities that come your way.

CONSCIOUSLY CURATE YOUR WARDROBE:

Approach your wardrobe with intention. Whether it's for a job interview, a corporate event, or a casual day, choose your outfits thoughtfully. Each item and accessory communicates a message about your commitment, attention to detail, and the value you place on your personal brand.

RECOGNISE THE POWER OF FIRST IMPRESSIONS AND UNDERSTAND THAT FIRST IMPRESSIONS ARE FORMED RAPIDLY, OFTEN IN A MATTER OF SECONDS:

Your appearance, body language and overall presentation contribute to these impressions. Acknowledge the psychological impact of your clothing choices and consider how they can help overcome any psychological barriers you face in various aspects of life, including work.

Chapter 6:

NEVER TRUST A MAN IN CROCS

Just like businesses carefully design their packaging to stand out on the shelves, individuals also craft their personal style as a unique and powerful representation of their personal brand identity. Well-designed packaging leaves a lasting impression on consumers and your personal style is your packaging that influences how people perceive you and it's what helps you stand out in a crowded world.

Embracing your unique traits and expressing them through your style sets you apart from the masses and makes you memorable. For years my signature style was largely identifiable by my pink pixie cut hair style, a skirt and T-shirt combo and a white pair of sneakers. As I mentioned in the last chapter, for others this can be a signature colour palette or statement accessories. Combining consistency and reality in your personal style and behaviour fosters authenticity, allowing others to connect with you on a deeper level. Over the years I have loved sharing style tips, hacks and outfit of the day #ootd inspiration on social media. However if you take a deeper look into my Instagram stories, for example, you will regularly find a very unmade up, real side to me at the gym five times a week.

There needs to be a balance between curating perfectly posed pictures and real life. By doing this you can also communicate your personal brand values – if you think about it brand packaging often conveys the values and principles of a company, and your personal style serves a similar purpose. Your style can communicate your beliefs, passions, and causes you support, helping you attract like-minded individuals and opportunities aligned with your values.

Never trust a man in Crocs

Super uncool back in the '90s when I was a child, Crocs somehow seem to have made a comeback and have even been designated as trendy and stylish, thanks Balenciaga! I would, however, never describe Crocs as either trendy or stylish, despite the number of people I see wearing them. I have also found to my cost and through experience that I would never trust a man (or woman for that matter) who turns up to a meeting in Crocs!

In 2009, not long after I published my first book, **Success in The City,** an email hit my inbox from a man who said he had bought my book at Dubai Duty Free on transit back home to Johannesburg, South Africa. His email said that he had been inspired by the stories I had written about successful Dubai-based entrepreneurs, and he had a proposition in mind which he felt could be mutually beneficial.

I'm not going to lie; I was quite flattered. I hadn't received any positive feedback from anyone outside my family and friends at this point. It's said that everyone has one good book in them. Writing and publishing a book is no small feat, so to learn that someone had taken the time to select my book and pay to read it was something of a "wow" moment for me.

He went on to share with me that he was a like-minded entrepreneur, with an idea. That idea was to take the concept of **Success in The City**, Dubai style, and roll it out to a relevant market in South Africa. He positioned himself as a co-author. Considering I have always had my sights set on global domination, I gave the proposition some serious thought. Perhaps, this was the universe showing me what my next step should be?

I'm a great believer that anything is possible, so what could go wrong with trying this market? Excited, I arranged to meet the gentleman during his next stopover in Dubai. Preparing carefully for my meeting, considering my personal brand, I meticulously planned not only my presentation, but what to wear. It was, after all, a business meeting with a potential partner. First impressions count, and I wanted to look the part.

Having only ever corresponded via email, I had no idea what he looked like. I had tried to undertake some background research and could find nothing. The more experienced me would have questioned this, but the somewhat naïve 29-year-old didn't.

When a man in baggy shorts, a T-shirt, and Crocs, yes, that's right Crocs (and socks) made a beeline across the hotel lobby towards me I was speechless, beyond words. He introduced himself as the man who wanted to co-author a book with me. Alarms were ringing in every corner of my brain.

It's not that I'm a harsh judge (that often) – I am all too aware that to judge a book by its cover should be a big no-no. In life, in general, this is good advice, because appearances can be deceiving and there is often more than meets the eye. However, the bottom line here was that this was a business meeting. His objective should have been to win me over, presenting convincingly as someone to be trusted, that he was credible, and we'd make a good partnership.

The reality is that we do judge. Our expectations of others are triggered not only by how they look, but how they present themselves overall. He most certainly hadn't dressed to impress. When is it ever acceptable for a grown man to turn up to a business meeting wearing Crocs? Perhaps on holiday you may find Crocs suitable attire, but to a meeting NEVER in my book.

I left the meeting with an uneasy feeling in the pit of my stomach. Was this really the type of person I wanted to work with? Was I being too judgmental? Just because his attire did not align with my personal values, was that reason enough to call a halt to our partnership? In my 20s I was on a mission to conquer the world. I wanted to build an empire, and I wasn't going to let a pair of Crocs get in my way. I took the plunge, booked a flight to South Africa, and it wasn't long before the cracks (or Crocs) started to appear.

Hindsight is always great; the warning signs were there. I had been too ready to believe. My lack of experience meant that I put my trust in him, believing that his intentions were good. They were not. He was most definitely not someone I wanted to work with.

Just days before I arrived in Johannesburg, I found myself waiting for him to share with me those participants who I would be interviewing for our joint venture. That brief had been clear. I had been assured at my initial Croc meeting that he had access to an extensive network, yet I had still to receive even one name.

I made a calculated decision to travel. As I touched down at OR Tambo International Airport, I was greeted by a text to say I had one interview the following day. That interview was one of the most awkward experiences of my career – my guest had no clear successful business concept to share. It was clear that Success in the City – The South African edition was not going to happen.

The idea of trying something may be daunting, but the benefits can be huge. In this instance I never heard from "the Croc Man" again. I learned to question more, delve beneath the exterior façade and trust my gut. That's the essence of lifelong learning – there is always more to discover. I took a flight to Cape Town, explored the beautiful landscape and found a vineyard to sit and sip wine on. Not all was bad!

> ## "FIRST IMPRESSIONS ARE LASTING; GIVE SPECIAL THOUGHT TO YOUR DRESS, YOUR GROOMING AND YOUR ACCESSORIES."
>
> — Brian Tracy, Canadian American motivational public speaker and self-development author

---

When was the last time you made the effort to deseed the lemon, take that extra effort and take action to audit what your current dress style is? Does your style contribute positively to your personal brand or not?

Having spent years working with clients specifically on this part of personal branding, I believe no style audit can be complete with an audit of your closet. Think of your closet like a kitchen pantry. A respectful chef will always carefully survey their ingredients before starting to cook; you need to look at your own ingredients – what is missing and what needs to be added in. Some ingredients may be past their sell by date and need to go.

An audit will determine what you are missing in the mix; a few simple basics to cook up a more casual look. You may be holding onto a pair of shoes that are comfortable, but well-worn; shabby and no longer chic.

If you're committed to transformational change, a serious style audit of your closet can take around three to four hours – that said it will depend upon the size of closet or closets you have. In my previous role as a celebrity stylist, I was never surprised by what might face me when I accepted a personal styling assignment. In Dubai, closets can be the size of a small house!

During your audit, identify items that are not pulling their weight, even if they still have their tags attached or are too small and hanging waiting for you to achieve your perfect weight – these have no place to hang around. You will need to be ruthless. If you are in doubt about how objective you can be, ask a friend and hopefully at the end of your audit you will remain friends.

Your closet should reflect who you are now and not what worked years ago, nor what you think might reflect who you are when you lose weight and fit into things. Change is the one constant in your life, your closet should evolve and fit with your life, no matter what stage you are at. Ultimately if you feel good, you will look good. If it's fit for purpose and represents your personal brand then keep it.

Your closet deserves a transformational make-over. Deseed the lemon, don't become irrevocably entrenched in an outdated closet, full of ill-fitting clothing that does not work for you.

TOP TIPS FOR A STYLE AUDIT

If you are looking for inspiration and focus, try my cheat sheet and ask yourself some simple questions.

- Does this even fit?
- Do you still wear it, or will you?
- Do you love it?
- Do you feel good in it?
- Does it fit with your lifestyle?
- Does it need to be altered before you can wear it? If so, get it altered or get rid of it.
- Does it work with other items in your closet, or would you need to buy new items to make use of it?
- How many interchangeable items do you own? If you have five pairs of jeans you are most likely not to wear your two least favourite pairs.
- Are you holding onto it for sentimental reasons? Be selective, only save what deserves a space in your closet.

The objective of a closet audit is that by the time you are ready to rehang your closet you can replace it in order, by lifestyle first, then outfit type. Start simple: work, weekend, workout, evenings out, holiday style. Adopt this practice and you will be able to clearly identify gaps in your closet. This makes it super easy to replenish or replace, either immediately or over time.

I've worked on this principle for over 20 years, both in my role as a celebrity stylist and latterly with my clients, as an intrinsic part of establishing their personal brand. Smaller, organised sections of your closet will ensure that you are no longer overwhelmed with too many choices and not the right style to promote the personal brand you are seeking to achieve.

Don't get me wrong, there is always room in your closet for the practical when it has a specific purpose. They will be classed as "Keep". I confess to making great use of a pair of hiking boots and padded trousers on a recent trip to Reykjavik, Iceland. They were not the most stylish items in my closet, but proved sensible and down-to-earth when faced with the ice and cold on a glacier walk.

You won't find me a big fan of the phrase "if you haven't worn it in six months, get rid of it". It's not an approach I tend to take with clients, it's far too wide a generalisation. Having made the Middle East my home for the past 20 years, I am all too aware that there are socio-economic and cultural constraints when it comes to style particularly. The Middle Eastern climate means that items from a closet may only be worn once a year and are likely to continue to be worn year in and out over a long period of time.

Reinvent the wheel, on average you wear 20 per cent of your closet 80 per cent of the time. How differently can you style a single item and with what you currently have in your closet?

I am a great advocate of Instagram, TikTok and Pinterest for style inspiration. For example, you've just bought yourself a pair of biker boots and want to find ways to incorporate them into your style. What could be easier than typing in "biker boots street style" and instantly you will see images pop up. You can choose how to emulate some of those looks that appeal to you using what you have in your own closet.

If you are looking for ideas of how to shape your style in a way that is right for your personal brand, use technology to your advantage. Using keywords like "style ideas", "street style" or "streetwear"; there is an abundant source of internet-based ideas to help you restyle your closet and tweak your look. You can create folders on your laptop or phone and save the looks you like and ways to style outfits. It's great to build up your ideal database for personal style.

Maximise your time and take photos of your outfits. How often have you forgotten what you have worn with what? Hands up! I am guilty of that too until Instagram story archives remind me of a post and I think, "wow I haven't worn that combo in ages." The beauty of taking a photograph of your outfit means you can also see, subjectively, the styled look. The practice will increase your confidence and awareness of your body. It will streamline your time to style as you look to hone your personal brand.

> ### *TOP TIP: UNCOVER YOUR PERSONAL BRAND STYLE*
>
> My top tip when you find yourself in the closet and looking for a deeper understanding of your personal brand style is to ask yourself these questions:
>
> - How would you describe the item? Crisp and tailored? Soft and ruffled?
> - What image does this item project? Smart and professional? Edgy and fashionable?
> - What colour is it? Does the shade compliment or clash with your complexion?
> - How does the silhouette hang? Nipped in at the waist? Flowing and hip-grazing?
> - What part of your body does it accentuate?
> - What part of your body does it de-emphasise?
> - How does it feel when you put it on? Does it fit?

Your closet should be functional! We are all prone to an impulse buy, but do your best to establish good choices and purchase what you know fits with your existing closet which is crafted to work for your personal brand.

When you buy an item, think can I make more than five different outfits from that choice? The next time you buy a new top or shirt, I challenge you to make five distinctive looks to wear it with. When you mix and match the same bottom with different tops, you will get a whole new outfit every time you change the top. People are less likely to notice that you have changed your look when you pair the same bottoms with different tops.

It will be the top item (not the bottom one) that will change the look of an outfit, giving a fresh and new angle. Not only can you create distinctive looks by simple pairing choices, you can also save money. There is no need to buy a new pair of jeans, trousers, or skirt when you combine them with a new top.

A recurring theme (signature style) is likely to appear as you audit your closet and current style. It's important to realise that your style and style personality can change over time. Whilst I have focused heavily in this chapter on talking about style, the relationship you have with your style is mirrored through your personal brand.

Your style personality is a combination of the traits of your personality, personal taste, and lifestyle. Your style personality enables you to communicate through your clothing choices. It can also be influenced by the seasons.

When I was training stylists and working with clients there was always a great interest in how your personality affects your style choices. Clothing choices include everything from top to toe, your hat to your shoes, and will include shape, cut, prints and colours. I was always less focused on body shapes, i.e. what you could and couldn't wear according to shape, concentrating instead on personality style – or my 5 Cs.

CLASSIC STYLE PERSONALITIES:

Tend to feel at their best in a more formal outfit. Well turned out, elegance is a key factor in their outfit choices. Their colour palate is most likely to be neutral tones, black or white. They may slip an occasional red or brown to wear. Classic hairstyles rarely change throughout their lives, the same goes for their outfits. You will always find them sporting a French or simple nail with very classic footwear.

CASUAL STYLE PERSONALITIES:

Tend to adopt outfits with simple lines, fabrics that are easy to care for and that don't need dry cleaning and minimal ironing. They look for outfits that make them feel comfortable. They are more likely to reach for a neutral, simple, easy to put on maxi dress for the summer, paired with simple sandals or sneakers. Their go-to is a simple T-shirt and denim for example.

CREATIVE STYLE PERSONALITIES:

Will have a closet full of items sourced from multiple origins. Vintage, mixed with designer or high street, bought online or in store. They love to shop, collecting and curating their closets. Not afraid of colour, mixing prints and trying different trends they will reinvent years later.

CAREFREE STYLE PERSONALITIES:

Are often seen as romantic in their styling, attracted to colourful florals, ruffled necklines or pleated skirts. They look for feminine fabrics, bow details and fringing.

"FASHION" CONSCIOUS STYLE PERSONALITIES:

Easily and quickly identified, the fashion conscious will be wearing whatever is "currently" in fashion regardless of whether it suits their body shape. Whether it's well-known labels or they're keen to be individual with up-and-coming designers, they will have a distinct personal brand.

Give it something extra

Accessories can play a significant role in making your personal brand stand out and leave a lasting impression on others. These seemingly small and often overlooked elements can have a powerful impact on how you are perceived and remembered. Accessories offer a unique opportunity to express your individuality and showcase your personality. Whether it's through bold statement pieces or subtle, meaningful items, your choice of accessories can communicate a lot about who you are and what you stand for, setting you apart from others.

Marie Morris, known as Mo, one of my previous clients, is the CEO of Morris Global Consulting and is a fashion and retail consultant. Her statement colourful accessories, from earrings to glasses and headwear, have become part of her personal brand identity.

Consistent accessories in your daily attire help create a cohesive personal brand image. When people see you regularly wearing a specific accessory or a signature piece, it becomes part of your recognisable style and reinforces your brand identity, not to mention that eye-catching or distinctive accessories can make you more memorable in the minds of others.

Paying attention to your accessories demonstrates your attention to detail and sense of style. For example, that could be a pocket square detail in a man's blazer. Thinking about your accessories shows that you care about how you present yourself, which can positively influence how others perceive your overall competence and professionalism. Standout accessories in particular can often become conversation starters. People may ask about the significance or story behind your accessory, giving you an opportunity to share more about yourself and your brand.

I have one client who has over 20 pairs of glasses, given that 90 per cent of the time he wears a thobe – a traditional garment worn by men in various Middle Eastern and North African countries. It is a long, loose-fitting robe, often white, that typically reaches down to the ankles and is characterised by its simplicity and modesty. Glasses have, therefore, become the detail that makes his personal brand different.

Some accessories may carry symbolic meaning or reflect your values and interests. For example, a bracelet from a charity organisation might demonstrate your commitment to a cause, or a unique necklace could represent a treasured memory. These symbols, including a tattoo, become part of your personal brand story.

Be mindful, at any given point in your life, you can change and evolve your style choices and your style personality. Rather than cling to the past, look to the future if you want to remain relevant. Deseed the lemon; examine your closet, remove every item. Take an assessment, look long and hard, and replace, according to lifestyle groupings, only what you know adds to your personal brand.

It's also important to consider colours in relation to your personal style, because the colours you choose to wear have a profound impact on your personal brand and how you feel. They communicate messages about your personality, values, and style. For instance, wearing bold and vibrant colours can convey confidence and creativity, while muted tones might suggest professionalism and reliability – it depends on your industry and what you like. Colour psychology is a powerful tool and much has been written on the subject in much more detail than I can cover here. The right colours can make you feel empowered, authentic, and capable of leaving a lasting, memorable impression, but there needs to be harmony between your wardrobe and your brand's logo. This is essential for ensuring consistency in visual identity.

It's important to note that everyone's personal brand is unique; there's no one-size-fits-all approach when it comes to style, hair and make-up choices. The key is to understand how you want to be perceived and ensure that your grooming and presentation align with the message you wish to convey about your personal brand.

I recently re-listened to a Tony Robbins CD, yes at the time of writing this book, my car still has one of these. He shared the story of how he was so close to signing one of his first big contracts and as he slid the pen over to the woman who he also admired, she slid the pen back and declared, looking at his fingernails which were all bitten and bloody, " I'm not going into business with someone who doesn't have the ability to stop biting their nails as an adult and doesn't take care of themselves." Call it harsh, but that was enough for Tony Robbins to disrupt the pattern in his brain and he finally stopped biting his nails, not to mention the humiliation.

Your personal brand style is a powerful tool that allows you to present yourself as a distinctive and valuable asset. Your success in personal branding lies in the ability to showcase your authentic self while cultivating a unique and desirable image. Embracing your personality and feeling confident in your choices are key ingredients in this transformative process. By aligning your personal style, behaviour, and communication (which we will discuss in the next chapter) with your true identity, you create a cohesive and authentic brand that stands out in the minds of others.

The more confidence you exude in embracing your personal brand style, the more it enhances your overall brand image, leaving a lasting and positive impression on those you encounter. Remember, how does your personal brand make people feel? Personal branding is an ongoing journey of self-discovery and refinement, empowering you to showcase the best version of yourself and unlock new opportunities along the way.

KEY PIP TAKEAWAYS

AUDIT YOUR PERSONAL STYLE AND CLOSET:

Take the time to evaluate your closet and personal style. Remove items that no longer align with your brand or lifestyle, and identify gaps that need to be filled. Curate a wardrobe that reflects your personality and values.

CHOOSE ACCESSORIES THOUGHTFULLY:

Accessories can make a significant impact on your personal brand. Select accessories that express your individuality and align with your personal brand message. Ensure they complement your outfits and help you stand out in a positive way.

PAY ATTENTION TO GROOMING:

Grooming plays a crucial role in personal branding. Ensure your hair and makeup choices reflect your style and personality. A well-groomed appearance signals professionalism and attention to detail.

FIRST IMPRESSIONS MATTER, ESPECIALLY IN BUSINESS SETTINGS:

Dress appropriately for meetings and professional encounters, and ensure your attire conveys credibility and trustworthiness.

EMBRACE CHANGE AND EVOLVE:

Personal branding is not static; it can evolve over time. Be open to embracing changes in your style and personality as you grow and evolve. Continuously refine your brand to remain relevant and authentic.

Chapter 7:

THE SUBSTANCE BEHIND THE STYLE

Style is defined in the Oxford Dictionary as being "a distinctive appearance". However, it is not only a distinctive appearance, but can also be something that you do in a particular manner or way.

Your personal brand style extends far beyond the clothes you wear or the words you speak. It encompasses the nonverbal cues you exude, such as body language, demeanour and presence. The way you carry yourself, your confidence and authenticity all contribute to the unspoken essence of your personal brand.

These nonverbal elements are equally powerful in shaping how others perceive and connect with you, making it essential to align every aspect of your presence to create a consistent and compelling personal brand image.

In 2005, I received an invite to feature in one of the Middle East's glossiest fashion magazines. I could barely contain my excitement. Media presence, the glossy kind where I could gain coverage for a new business enterprise, was priceless. Given it was for a high-end fashion focused publication, it was perfect to debut my personal shopping and styling business.

I thought long and hard about how best to present my new business. Correspondence between the journalist and I over email was warm and engaging. I was really looking forward to meeting her and for her to join me on one of my most luxurious shopping and styling services that I offered at the time.

The luxury experience: a limo transfer to Dubai's most opulent shopping mall, an exclusive shopping and styling session in preselected boutiques followed by sunset drinks in one of Dubai's top rooftop bars. For that occasion, I plumped for a venue overlooking The Palm, Jumeirah, the man-made island shaped like an enormous palm tree which was only just beginning to plant its fashionable roots with luxury apartments and hotels. Her brief, to document the experience.

I was ready to deseed the lemon; to make sure that every moment of her time spent with me exceeded her expectations. On meeting the journalist, I detected none of the previous warmth exuded in our earlier email correspondence, to the point where I wondered if I had maybe been assigned a different journalist. Her personal brand was somewhat lacking, she was sultry, bordering rude and totally disinterested. Was this the same person that I had been talking to on email?

If nothing else I am tenacious. I exuded high energy compensating for the lack of hers, determined to offer what is always my best version of self. I was though equally concerned that she would not document her experience in a positive light. By the end of the very long day, I was drained. I did, however, take the time to check that the journalist who had joined me was the same as the writer of the emails, she was!

As I waited with trepidation for the article to hit print, I found to my surprise and great relief that it read with the same warmth, engagement and positivity that we'd had on our much earlier email exchanges. So why was she so different in person? I put it down to the fact that she was having an off day, after all we all have them. That said, in the following years, in all my personal interactions with her she behaved in the same manner – her behind-the-scenes email exchanges continued to exude warmth, yet her face-to-face remained wanting. It was just how she exhibited her personal brand.

Always remember, your personal brand is not just what people see or hear; it's how you make them feel. Leave an indelible impression through genuine connections and warm interactions, for that is what truly defines your brand's essence.

Understand your cues

Whether it's a great email communication style or the opposite, either way this sets the tone for your personal brand. Vanessa Van Edwards, a communication expert and bestselling author, shares in her latest book **CUES: Master the Secret Language of Charismatic Communication** how to convey charisma, power, trust and likability in any situation. She talks about how the tiny signals you're sending – from your stance and facial expressions to your word choice and vocal tone – can affect your personal brand and communication style.

Vanessa shares cues that are the powerful verbal, non-verbal and vocal signals humans send to one another. Social messages convey hidden information about the people you spend time with. She groups "cues" into four key categories:

1. **Nonverbal cues**: Your body language, posture, gestures and facial expressions.
2. **Vocal cues:** Your cadence, pace, volume and speaking tone.
3. **Verbal cues:** The words you use in person, in email, in text or on the phone.
4. **Imagery cues:** The colours you wear, your ornaments and the props you use in your home, desk, office photo and video backgrounds.[7]

---

[7] Vanessa Van Edwards, (2022), *Cues: Master the Secret Language of Charismatic Communication*, Penguin Business, 1st edition

Cues can enhance or weaken your message. How you talk, how and where you stand, the colours that you wear, your facial expressions, what you do with your hands, where you gaze and how you say hello on the phone can either be seen as positive or negative interactions.

They can even come down to what emojis you use in your email, text and WhatsApp exchanges, which Vanessa shares are a great warmth cue.

After years of ground-breaking academic research, Vanessa has been able to narrow down how you can recognise cues successfully.

It's a simple equation: Charisma = Warmth + Competence.

I encourage you, if you are serious about personal branding (and you should be if you are ready to deseed the lemon), to follow Vanessa's audit exercise, where she invites you to look at your last five emails sent and count how many warm and competent cues you have used. This is your opportunity to act and deseed the lemon – how have your most recent emails made your recipients feel?

Focus on your body language

From verbal to non-verbal cues, it's important that you do not underestimate the importance of attending to every little detail. There is power behind your presentation, and your body language is a keen driver in how others will perceive you.

Back in 2012, Amy Cuddy, a social psychologist and author, made TED history by garnering 69 million views to date and becoming the second most popular TED talk of all time when she presented her research on the benefits of power posing.[8]

It is her belief that by commanding a powerful stance and adopting a high-power pose (or expansive posture), you can make yourself feel more powerful and thus act with more self-confidence. She says that our body language can dictate how we think and feel about ourselves. How you choose to hold and move your body can, in turn, impact your mind. Formidable thoughts indeed.

It makes complete sense to me. What kind of a first impression would you be giving if you offered up a limp handshake, avoided eye contact, or you sat slumped over your desk? It wouldn't impart a great feeling of confidence to me.

What would be the difference if you proffered a firm handshake, had great eye contact, or sat at your desk in a confident manner? You would demonstrate confidence, and come across as someone who others want to engage and work with.

Of course, there are always hidden internal cues – the person that you find standing in front of you will have no idea what is going on inside your mind. Perhaps you have

---

[8] Cuddy, A. (no date) *Your body language may shape who you are.* https://www.ted.com/talks/amy_cuddy_your_body_language_may_shape_who_you_are?language=en.

had a recent bereavement, a family member is very sick, or you have maxed out your credit card and are wondering how to meet the monthly payment.

Whoever is forming a first impression of you is unlikely to know about any personal struggles you may be facing. All they see is the external cues you are demonstrating. You have the power to control this; it's in your own hands to present yourself in a manner which reflects your personal brand.

As a keynote speaker, I have worked with a considerable number of luxury hotels delivering my 'Deseed the Lemon' talk. The hospitality industry has also been a perfect platform for me where I get to host practical workshops for management and their teams.

The reason my message resonates so well with the hospitality industry is that it is fundamentally about people serving people. It is, however, not just about service; it's about offering a unique and memorable experience.

First impressions matter. Employees are the front-line representatives of the brand, who directly interact with guests. They are the first port of call. An overall guest experience can and will be impacted by the personality, behaviour, and personal brand of an employee. In this incredibly competitive environment, I work with employees to harness their power and show them where they can influence a strong personal brand that will set themselves apart from others.

In 2018 I was approached by a luxury hotel based in Abu Dhabi, the UAE's capital. Their brief was to create a consistent personal brand standard for their employees that would enhance the hotel brand. Employees are, after all, walking, talking billboards! This hotel brand recognised that employees with personal brands were an asset for them as employers. They wanted to create a culture where their employees would stay front of mind, create an expert profile and deliver the WOW factor.

With many hotels leaning away from traditional corporate style uniforms to allow space for employees to be more individual, it can create a myriad of looks, styles and ways and manners of doing things that are often not seen as a 5-star offering.

One area, in addition to personal style and grooming, that I was asked to address was meet and greet – the "wet fish" handshake that hotel guests were being greeted with. For those of you who have yet to experience the wet fish handshake, it's one of the worst handshakes in the world – limp, listless and just a tad wet. Sure, you don't want to have a bone crusher handshake, but the wet fish handshake is considered to be poor personal brand etiquette. It can be perceived as a sign of disinterest, lack of confidence, sometimes even insincerity. Put more simply, it fails to convey professionalism and trust, crucial qualities when establishing positive connections with others, personally or professionally.

Your handshake is an essential aspect of nonverbal communication and very often the first impression when meeting someone new. You want a firm and confident handshake, which is generally regarded as a sign of respect, engagement and a willingness to connect.

Don't forget about your verbal handshake

So, if your physical handshake delivers a powerful message about your trustworthiness and level of interest in the other person, what does your verbal handshake say? A verbal handshake can be most easily described as the way you answer your phone.

As children, my sister, Mhairi, and I were frequently called out by our school friends. My mum instilled in us at a very early age her telephone etiquette. We were never allowed to answer the phone with a simple "Hello." We always answered by saying, "Hello, this is Kelly speaking." It always amused my friends to no end. Who would have thought that back in the '80s my mum was practising personal branding?

Understanding your communication style and auditing will require you to step back and reflect. A lack of awareness over how your communication style impacts others can have a detrimental impact on your personal brand. Through time you can very often default to habitual communication patterns, which you may have developed without conscious thought.

You may be oblivious to the fact that you need to evaluate or change your communication style, particularly if you have grown comfortable with the way you communicate. That's not to say that your style is not right or cannot be elevated. You can deseed the lemon and in doing so gain valuable insight into whether your communication style is holding your personal brand back and identify what areas you can improve on.

As a brand strategist, when I work with clients, I ask them to take part in an anonymous personal brand audit, as I mentioned in Chapter 2. This transparent process represents an opportunity for my clients to ask family, friends and colleagues to give valuable feedback about how their brand is seen.

You may see yourself as motivational, articulate, friendly, educated, powerful, knowledgeable, helpful, nurturing, serious, fun or energetic. How you sound to others may be in direct correlation. Words should echo how you are portrayed across your social media platforms. Start with the "sound" you wish to project with your personal brand. What do you want your sound to convey?

How does your personal brand feel and what do you want people to see you as? You may be looking to project that you are inspirational, motivated, authentic, approachable or thoughtful. You may be looking to project as educational, ethical, sustainable, innovative or impactful. Or simply, focused, kind, happy and family focused.

It's important, with all this investment in your personal brand, not to take your eye off the ball. You can easily damage your personal brand nonverbally when your actions or behaviours negatively impact how others perceive you, eroding both built-up trust and credibility.

Other communication red flags

There are many other red flags you can pick up on when it comes to communication. Being mindful of these ensures that you don't fly these red flags for others to see.

For example, in my early days of business, I often found myself in the difficult position of getting suppliers and, dare I say it honestly, clients to pay their invoices. Not paying on time is a red flag! A sign of lack of integrity, unreliability and poor financial management. It tarnishes reputations and damages relationships, as I learned to my cost. I always settle my invoices promptly and pay my team on time; treat people how you want to be treated.

Another red flag is bad manners. Basic good manners show those around you that you respect others and are considerate to their feelings. Being disrespectful or rude towards others, regardless of whether it's family, friends, colleagues or clients, creates a negative impression and will hinder collaboration and cooperation. Ghosting is a classic example. Ignoring or choosing not to respond to someone's texts or emails is poor personal branding. No one likes to be on the receiving end of this. I find this practice rude and disheartening – it reflects poorly on the people who ghost and the companies that they work for.

Many of my clients confess to me that they have had first-hand experience of ghosting. I too have been subjected to this quite recently by an employee of a PR company in Dubai, who reached out to me to collaborate with a luxury hotel chain. Having called me and discussed their brief I submitted my proposal by email, as requested, and waited.

I waited some more, then followed up not just once but twice. They failed to respond to my email and to my subsequent call. Their lack of courtesy to end communication either way is quite frankly poor form and does nothing to enhance a personal brand.

Clients of mine get very disheartened in the early days when someone takes interest in their product or service, then goes cold never to be heard from again. Ghosting can easily demolish a business' reputation, and it's bad for your personal brand if you do it to others. Treat others how you would like to be treated yourself. If you don't want to be invisible, don't treat others like they are.

Communication red flags aren't only what people don't do, but also how you respond to their communications with you. Feedback or criticism can be constructive and should not be ignored without considering its merits. It demonstrates an unwillingness to learn and grow, deterring potential clients, partners or employers.

The bottom line is, communication matters. Inconsistent or unreliable communication so often leads to misunderstandings and creates a perception of unreliability and disorganisation. It's important to remember too that gossip is never healthy and spreading negativity about others will reflect poorly on your brand – not to mention creating a toxic environment.

When you commit, stay the course. Failing to follow through on promises or commitments can damage trust and make others hesitant to rely on your word or work. I'm a stickler for ethical practices, and here in the Middle

The Substance Behind the Style

East, there is no room for displaying unethical behaviour. Lying, cheating or manipulation all have a great cost, can severely harm your personal brand and lead to irreparable damage to your reputation. Not to mention worse.

That said, we all make mistakes! When you do, own them, don't deflect the blame. When you own your mistakes, you demonstrate integrity and accountability. Owning up shows others that you are willing to take responsibility and grow from these experiences.

Your personal brand is formed by the perception others have of you based on your actions, behaviour and values. Building and maintaining a strong personal brand requires consistent effort to ensure your actions align with the image you want to project.

Your personal brand reflects how you make others feel and the impression you leave on them. By being mindful of your communication style and ethical conduct, you can build a strong and authentic personal brand that resonates with others and fosters positive connections. Be aware of others' feelings, empathy costs nothing and goes a long way to building strong relationships.

KEY PIP TAKEAWAYS

TAKE A PERSONAL BRAND STYLE AUDIT:

Take a personal brand style audit to understand your personal brand style, which includes both verbal and nonverbal cues. Reflect on how you come across to others through your body language, tone of voice, choice of words, appearance and overall demeanour. Identify inconsistencies between the image you want to project and how you are perceived by others.

EXPAND YOUR COMMUNICATION CUES:

To do so, assess your verbal, nonverbal, vocal and imagery cues to ensure they align with the impression you want to create. Think Charisma = Warmth + Competence. Details matter, so pay attention to your email communication, handshake and overall body language to create a positive and impactful first impression.

BE MINDFUL TO UPHOLD ETHICAL STANDARDS IN YOUR ACTIONS AND INTERACTIONS:

Be respectful, demonstrate accountability and be empathetic in your dealings with others. Avoid engaging in gossip, spreading negativity or disregarding commitments, as these actions can damage your personal brand and reputation.

Deseed The Lemon

SLICE THREE:

STATIONERY

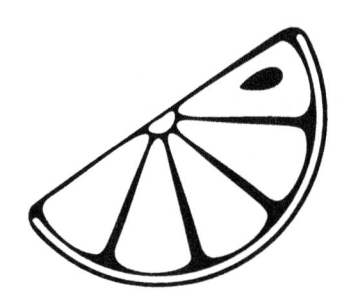

Stationery might conjure up a vision of a desk full of pens and pencils (branded of course), a stapler or paperweight to name but a few. What I mean when referring to stationery in this slice is your collateral touchpoints that represent your personal brand – creative assets designed to promote your personal brand and business. They communicate why potential and existing clients should choose your product or service above any other.

Your brand collateral should match your standards of business and communicate effectively, and consistently, using verbal and visual design. Everything from a thoughtful thank you card you send to a client, to printed brochures, ebooks, newsletters, graphics and even the CV you present for your next job, represent your collateral. It also extends to great photography, that could get you featured in **Vogue** (like Winnie), and a website that excels in the collection of leads and closing of sales.

Brand collateral, or what I typically refer to as Slice Three: Stationery, is all about getting your personal brand noticed and strengthening the bond between you and your clients. Well-designed and thought-out stationery will help to increase engagement with your clients and build connections with people at every stage of their journey with you. It's essential to developing loyal fans who sing your praises about just how great your brand is.

Each touch point can make or break the perception that someone has of you. It is the art of deseeding the lemon. This goes beyond stationery in the traditional sense of the word – it extends to the entirety of your personal brand's visual identity. This visual identity should be

Slice Three: Stationery

carried through all the content you share. You should make this clean and clear. Doing so will help you to discover your target audience, your visual aesthetics. It will be the substance to create guidelines around your brand. Smart choices will keep you accountable for decisions, like logo colours and captions on social media.

Chapter 8:

WHAT IS STATIONERY AND WHY IT MATTERS

As I explained in the introduction to this Slice, stationery encompasses physical items as well as your brand's visual identity. Let's start by exploring the physical elements of stationery and how they can benefit you.

Everyone loves a freebie!

I feel sure that either in your home or your office you have at least one freebie that you have picked up or there's an email that hits your inbox because you signed up for it in exchange for some form or information. It may be a branded mug, pen, pencil or memory stick, the results of a quiz that you took or even a free ebook.

A survey conducted by MagicFreebiesUK found that 60 per cent of consumers purchased products or services because of signing up for a free trial or sample – "a freebie".[9] They can go a long way to building your brand image.

If you want to be a leader in your field of expertise, offering freebies can create a reputation of giving back and rewarding your clients for loyalty. If you want to differentiate yourself from your competitors, offering freebies is a positive way to help you attract people and for you to grow a valuable database. Think of it as bums on seats!

Knowing who your real audience is matters. When your clients request a freebie, you can build a valuable, up-to-date database of consumers who are interested in you and your services, and you can leverage this information for future growth.

Giving away a freebie could involve costs for you which may seem a little daunting at the outset, but remember that a freebie gives you the opportunity to engage with potential customers and promote your presence. You may feel that you don't have the budget, or are not quite ready to commit to such an outlay. However, there are creative ways in which you can offer a freebie without breaking the bank.

For example, downloadable printable planners could help your audience meet their goals, just customise your

---

9 *How Offering Freebies And Discounts Can Act As A Powerful Marketing Tool And Increase Sales Revenue* (no date). https://www.freshbusinessthinking.com/purpose/how-offering-freebies-and-discounts-can-act-as-a-powerful-marketing-tool-and-increase-sales-revenue/3102.article.

printables to match your brand. Other options include digital downloads that share your experience, vouchers for your services or a free masterclass to share your knowledge. These have no cost to you, but are creative ways to enhance your visibility without breaking the bank.

If you have a small budget to spend, you might want to consider investing in sustainable products to offer new clients like a reusable tote bag. Back in Edinburgh I attended an event in the summer when I found the need to use an umbrella – the one I had to hand was a freebie from a company I had worked with.

Janara Jones, designer and speaker, is a great example of how to utilise this approach. She has bright yellow tote bags that consumers get when they buy one of her products. The tote bags are sustainable as they can get reused multiple times – recycling at its very best. Her bags are very often photographed and can be seen all over social media. Items like this are practical, trendy and appeal to a wide audience.

I give all my clients a framed card with a special quote and on the back is space where they can write their goals and frame them, then they have the option to use the quote card after they have achieved their goals. At my mastermind I give out branded pens, which are also sustainably sourced. It's a win-win!

Learning the power of branded collateral

My first branded collateral was a simple piece of stationery – a résumé (CV) of my experience – designed to market me. I was 14 years old when I put this together. As a child of the '80s, I was the first one in my class to have divorced parents.

With all that was going on with my parents as they made their difficult decisions, I didn't want to add to their worries. Not that pocket money was an issue, but I felt it was the right time to start thinking about getting a weekend job. I felt a sense of responsibility to ease some of my mum's worries, or share her load, albeit in some very small way.

At 14, I hadn't banked on the UKs limiting employment legislation and the restrictions that made it almost impossible to secure anything other than a paper round. I knew I didn't want to go down that road. Whilst early mornings have never been an issue for me, the dreich weather of Scotland – wet, dull, gloomy, dismal, dreary – has always been a challenge for me to contend with and I wanted to limit my exposure to those dull and dismal Scottish weather conditions as much as possible.

I found it to be a competitive employment market even at the age of 14. Finding a suitable job that would work around school studies and hockey playing was no easy feat. Where to start. Never daunted and always with the belief that anything is possible when you set your mind to it, I set about my objective to secure a job.

I figured that a Saturday girl in a hair salon would be the most suitable route. I located the Yellow Pages, a good old fashioned and somewhat large telephone directory for local businesses, and began my search.

After making a list of hair salons in Edinburgh, I decided that the personal touch was far better than making a telephone call. As my list began to form, I gave thought to what might make me stand out and appeal to a salon. How could I differentiate myself from others also trying to find Saturday employment at 14 years old?

"First impressions are everything, Kelly," said my mum. Even today, many years later, her advice rings true. Rather than just turning up on salon doorsteps furnished with nothing more than my charm, mum insisted that I should present a professional image at the outset. She helped me craft my very first CV to take with me to share with each of the salons I had shortlisted – one of the main criteria for my shortlist was that I knew each would employ someone under the age of 16. At the ripe old age of 14, I didn't have much to put in my résumé (not a great wealth of life experience), but that didn't stop my mum from identifying what she determined was my personal brand and putting those thoughts into writing.

We were able to construct a compelling account of what I had done to date – after all, I had already perfected the art of making hot water with lemon, not quite tea, and I always managed to wash and straighten my hair to look pristine. Combined with my passion and drive to get my very first job I felt I was on a winner, and it worked. After handing over my professional, one-page, typed résumé to many salons, I finally landed an interview and was offered a job washing hair with Chris Dixon at Dixon Reid in Edinburgh.

In some situations, the first impression that people will have of you may very well not be you as the front-facing person, it will be what they see online. From a website to the first email you send, social media or the lack of it – this all creates a perception of who you are.

I've come a long way from the little girl who used to swing on the garden gate shouting "hello" to anyone that was walking by. It is my belief that by working in front-facing customer service environments at such a young age I was able to hone my skills to a level where they have had a profound impact on my career and ability to operate successful global businesses.

That CV and my first work experience with Chris sowed the seeds for further employment. This encompasses everything from working overseas with Direct Holidays as their youngest-ever holiday rep, being cabin crew with Emirates, arriving in Dubai as the Iraq War erupted and eventually stepping into entrepreneurship launching my first business, StyleMeDivine, located in Dubai, followed by launching two more businesses to date. Every experience has given me a story to share.

With the effective art of communication, I have the ability to relate to and work with people of all nationalities. I thrive in a multicultural and diverse environment, whether that means I'm talking to holidaymakers abroad, travellers en route to worldwide destinations, business owners, CEOs or budding entrepreneurs. My early experiences and those to date have not only equipped me with the ability to articulate effectively, but also nurtured my empathy and adaptability.

Those experiences working for others and running my own business all went into packaging my personal brand as Kelly Lundberg, personal brand strategist with a flagship business: Brand YOU Creators, where I'm working with entrepreneurs, corporate companies and some of the leading luxury brands in the world – I did say anything was possible. If you are serious about pivoting your personal brand, it pays to develop your stationery and take the time to consider what to focus on and how you can deseed the lemon successfully.

Having the right stationery, or collateral, helps to share crucial information about what you do, and your products and services, with your audience. When a client signs up to work with me, they need to be able to relate to my brand. They need to like what they see in my "shop window" and be able to relate to what they see as my values and beliefs.

I am a big fan of digital and print collateral which goes a long way to engage with potential clients and organisations. Effective print collateral can provide powerful leverage in today's digital world as printed communication about your brand can leave a lasting impression on those you meet. It offers a tangible message and promotes your products and services. A professional website, signature email, branded colours and fonts and quality photographs also determine your professional status and form a lasting first impression.

The following are the most important things to consider when it comes to your stationery and brand collateral in today's world.

Own your own domain name

This will be your IP and part of your personal brand equity – you never know what you might need it for. It's fairly inexpensive to purchase, sometimes as cheap as 20 pence, depending on how common your name is. This investment can be the best purchase you ever make as you start to build your personal brand name.

In 2009, I tried to buy my domain name: kellylundberg.com. My name isn't the most common so you can imagine my surprise even back then when it was not available. In my despair I paid for a broker to find out who owned it and several emails later I had established contact. I explained to the owner of kellylundberg.com that I was in the early stages of building my personal brand and would like to buy the domain name from him to keep my social media handles consistent, but he point blank refused.

I wanted to be mad at the gentleman for refusing the sale, but I saw reason when he told me that he had a new baby daughter who was named Kelly Lundberg and he wanted to gift her the legacy of her domain name in time. He obviously had the foresight and a business mind; I was mad at my parents for not having done the same. Only kidding mum and dad, in fairness when I was a kid I don't think domain names even really existed!

Having to change tack swiftly I opted, at the time, for what everyone in Dubai said was going to be the next big thing and bought the domain name kellylundberg.co. I quickly learnt the error of my ways. After spending some time as a celebrity stylist in Los Angeles, then in London, I saw how I'd inadvertently created confusion. In the United States everyone assumed that I was .com, and in the UK that I was a .uk domain. When I handed out my business cards and flyers, eager recipients were keen to point out what they thought was a spelling mistake.

It wasn't until 2017 that I made the bold decision to update my personal brand website so that I could benefit from having the same name on social media handles as my website. Remember what I said earlier – consistency is key. Making sure your personal brand identity is consistent over all digital platforms is the real imperative.

I have not been alone when making such decisions. When Instagram first launched, popular influencers rose to the top of their game using quirky and eye-catching names. In 2009, an Italian blogger, businesswoman, fashion designer and model introduced herself to her Instagram followers as @theblondsalad. In 2017 she rebranded as herself @chiaraferragni earning herself the title then of number one fashion influencer. She shares not only her professional life, but also stories of her personal life and strives to be authentic.

Similarly, @Travelinhershoes started to share her passion for people and culture though her Instagram. She too has more recently rebranded under her name @aggie. Many others have followed. In 2015, reality TV star Kylie (Jenner) filed papers with the United States Patent and Trademark Office (USPTO) to trademark KYLIE for advertising and endorsement services in the United States. Jenner was blocked by the Australian pop star Kylie Minogue.

Jenner has always remained silent about the decision, but Minogue, in an appearance on **Watch What Happens Live,** said "I've spent a lifetime protecting me and building my brand so it was something that had to be done."[10]

Making a name change can be a tough decision, but there are many reasons why you might choose to do so. Nothing stays constant, we all change over time. It might be that your looks, your passion, or your goals change. It's unreasonable to think personal brands can stay the same forever. I think it is reasonable to be looking for ways to reinvent and reimagine yourself.

However, there are times when changing your public persona isn't the best course of action, even if things in your personal life have changed. For example, I once interviewed Pippa Kenton-Page, an Olympic gold medallist, for one of my podcasts. Before the recording, I set out to do some research. I always like to start at the natural place and "Google" an individual I am working with or am about to work with. But I could find nothing about her, not one thing. After we'd been introduced on the day of the interview I confessed that I knew next to nothing about

---

10   Watch What Happens Live with Andy Cohen (2022) *Kylie Minogue's trademark battle against Kylie Jenner* | WWHL. https://www.youtube.com/watch?v=HX2C5bLjao4.

her background as my research had revealed nothing about her, yet she came highly recommended. It turned out that she had won her Olympic medal under her maiden name. Suddenly it all made sense. She filled me in on her story and we had a great interview.

Although in Chapter 2 I said you'd be unlikely to do business with someone who has no social media presence, there are exceptions to this rule – as this example shows. In this instance, the person in question had come recommended by someone I trusted, not to mention that my interest had been piqued and I was keen to explore her story further.

As with the Olympic gold medallist who went under her maiden name, I have worked with other clients who have kept their married name following divorce. Their reason for this was that they felt their identity had been established under their then-married name rather than their maiden name. They still work successfully under those established personal brands.

Another challenge with names can come if you have a name that is difficult to pronounce or spell. I know this all too well. Having been born in Edinburgh, Scotland, I stay true to my Scottish heritage, despite my unusual Swedish surname, Lundberg. Growing up and all through my school days I always felt different. I didn't quite fit in with the traditional McKenzies, Frasers, Campbells and Stewarts. I was teased mercilessly about my name. Kids can be so cruel!

One Sunday visit to my grandparents, in floods of tears, I told my Granda that nobody could pronounce my surname correctly and that I was constantly made fun of. Now, my Granda was not a cuddly man or even particularly approachable; he was a businessman working in a predominantly man's world of shipping, that never changed.

Granda was a great thinker, and he didn't have lots to say to his grandkids, but I do remember quite clearly what he said to me that Sunday. "Your own name is distinctive. Use it to create your unique identity. It may be hard just now but your name is so specific it will help people remember your business, for all the right reasons." Some 30 years later I understand.

The United Arab Emirates is a cultural melting pot. My clients in search of defining their personal brand are eclectic, only a few have their origins from the UAE, but many have chosen this city as their home. One such client hails from Turkey and has a very unusual first name, Öykü. She shared with me that people she met found it very difficult to pronounce her name, nigh on impossible at times. She wanted to simplify. Reflecting on my Granda's words of wisdom I suggested that she embrace her name, but use tools like LinkedIn where you can add name pronunciation.

Öykü quickly learned that by creating a recording of how her name was pronounced and adding it to her profile she could herself stay true to her name. At Brand YOU Creators we have been able to offer the same option on her personal branded website. Simple yet a game changer.

One final point on names – beware of nicknames. If you are serious about building your online authority to become well-known in your space or industry, you may want to consider the value of your own name.

During a recent conversation with an individual looking for my help with their personal brand strategy, it transpired that they had been using a nickname as their personal brand, but their professional journey had recently led them to collaborate with government officials. This transition raised concerns. Was the nickname professional enough to continue with as their evolving persona in this new context? My answer was no and I suggested this person needed to change their nickname to their real name.

Your email address matters

Avoid, at all costs, making business connections from your personal email accounts, like Gmail or Hotmail. There is nothing that says you are not taking your business seriously more than using a personal email account.

In the same vein, make sure you have a professional email signature. When there is no email signature on the bottom of correspondence you should question just how legit a person is. It has no substance. Personally, I tend to delete any unsolicited and unbranded approaches. I'm sure I'm not alone, so if you don't already have an email signature, just consider the harm you could be doing to your personal brand and, by extension, your business.

A website

This is your "shop window" to your personal brand, and very often the first impression of you is made here. Websites don't need to be complicated and can fit every possible budget. A simple single page can still showcase you – if it says who you are and how to reach you, it will establish trust and credibility. Keep in mind that if someone cannot find any relevant information relating to you, they are more than likely to assume that you are no expert in your field of expertise.

To attract, you need to be able to succinctly articulate what you offer. Drive traffic to your website by getting people to sign up for your newsletter or via quizzes and media links. Keep any links current. Links can, at times and for various reasons, disconnect so always audit your website for working links regularly. Remember the key – consistency!

From time to time, I'm approached by companies asking me to join them as a guest. Invitations with a Scottish twist are always something that I am keen to support. Macallan Whisky asked me to join them for a private dining experience.

I found myself sitting next to the then newly appointed deputy editor from **Harper's Bazaar, Arabia**, Jessica Michault. As we chatted together, I discovered that Jessica had only recently arrived in Dubai. Originally from the USA she had spent several years in Paris, where she had learned French fluently.

New to Dubai, I asked her about her experience of securing a role in the Middle East. Her response was refreshing. She told me that over the years she had invested heavily in her personal brand to be seen as an educator, influencer and thought leader in the fashion industry. Her investment included the design and launch of a personal website with thought leader articles contributing to her online presence which gave her the visibility and voice to be seen by a larger audience. Ultimately it was this that led to her new role in the Middle East. It proves the point that a personal brand is not just the domain of entrepreneurs and business owners, it can be leveraged in a corporate environment too.

Business cards

Digital or paper-based, a business card can often be the first interaction prospective clients will have with your brand, so make sure it's a positive one that increases your personal brand perception and exposure.

Some will agree that a thick business card signals luxury and captures attention quickly. Others will argue they are not sustainable or environmentally friendly. First impressions are important, so you must decide which world you sit in with your personal brand values and make sure these align with your ideal clients. Your business card says a lot about you so be sure to choose a design that reflects your brand.

While there are those who won't forgo a physical business card, Covid-19 has changed a lot. There is nothing like a global pandemic to make us all rethink how we do business. A physical presence has been replaced by an intangible digital presence in many cases, but this isn't without its advantages.

At a recent conference, whilst I did have business cards, I didn't share any as everyone connected using the conference QR code on LinkedIn. Once an attendee had logged into the portal and made a digital connection, it sent a personal meet and greet and allowed those attending to keep conversations alive long after the initial introductions had taken place. This would not have happened using a conventional business card.

Flyers and booklets

Creative flyers and booklets detailing your personal brand and business should focus on clear messaging supported by attractive visuals. Eye-catching designs can capture people's attention and encourage them to engage with not only your content, but can result in better sales too. High-quality and well-designed flyers and booklets give a professional impression to your target audience. They show that you care about the presentation of your content and are willing to invest in creating a positive experience for your customers or clients.

I've used many of my flyers and booklets as part of my marketing toolkit and have taken them on photoshoots with me, which in turn have been used in adverts across social media. If you do in-person events or connect with the local community, these pieces of collateral help to build your offline personal brand persona.

Thank you cards/cue cards

Personally branded thank you cards are an asset to have in your personal branding stationery toolkit. Not only is it memorable and unique, sending a personally branded thank you card sets you apart from generic thank you messages. A handwritten thank you card also demonstrates your genuine gratitude and thoughtfulness. It shows that you took the time and effort to express your thanks in a personal and meaningful way. Subtly promoting your brand, it reminds recipients of your expertise and services, potentially leading to referrals or new opportunities.

But what I truly love is expressing gratitude through thank you cards and in doing so boosting my mood and overall mental wellbeing. The act of saying "thank you" fosters a positive and appreciative mindset, so it benefits you personally, as well as being a great way to stay front-of-mind with your customers.

I've used my personally branded thank you cards as cue cards at public speaking events too. Cue cards have always been an important part of my collateral, particularly in my early days of speaking at events or hosting panel discussions. The cards themselves can act as my roadmap, helping me remember key information and stay on track when I'm speaking. However, I like to make my cue cards multipurpose. This means they're branded A5 cards that can also serve as thank you notes – which are always handwritten – during the event.

Packaging

This plays a crucial role in enhancing your brand's image and positively impacting your business. With packaging, we're going back to the fundamentals where first impressions count. Packaging allows you to display your product or service in the best-possible light. It's often the first thing your clients will see before making a purchase. A well-designed and visually appealing package entices your audience to explore further.

When I first launched my personal styling agency, I had luxury branded StyleMeDivine carrier bags designed. As much as I was offering a service, I found that clients often purchased gift cards for friends or family members. I would package up a carefully crafted gift receipt and tie it to a padded coat hanger with a printed ribbon, ready for their first purchase with me to hang on. The bag, gift receipt and ribbon were all unique and packaged with my brand logo. They were easily recognisable because of the consistent use of colour and brand logo font. While visuals enhance brand recognition; packaging can also communicate brand values and personality.

Not all service businesses will need packaging, but there are many elements that can be classed as packaging for your offerings. For example, you may have a requirement for packaging for sending welcome kits to new clients. These kits might include instructional guides, access codes and promotional materials. Presentation folders can help you organise and present documents, reports and proposals in a polished and organised manner. If you offer training or educational services, you may need to provide course materials, workbooks, or training manuals in some form of packaging, or send marketing collateral like brochures, posters, or promotional items to clients. If your service includes gift certificates or vouchers for gifting purposes, consider packaging them attractively to make them more gift-worthy.

In today's ever-evolving environment, ecofriendly packaging, for example, reflects a commitment to sustainability, which can resonate with environmentally conscious consumers. One such client of mine, Sandhya Lalloo-Morara, founded the Ido movement in 2020 – her clothing label was directly correlated to her desire to fashion a sustainable lifestyle brand. Her passion is brands and products which can foster an emotional connection. Sandhya is all about reducing the carbon footprint, so the clothing she offers is made from collections of recycled plastic bottles, fishing nets and organic fabrics such as hemp and bamboo. Her sustainable lifestyle brand directs her consumers to plant the seed labels attached to her clothing and watch the plants grow, provided, of course, you care for them well.

Likewise, the digital age has seen a rise in unboxing experiences, with cult followings on Instagram, TikTok and YouTube. "Unboxing" has become an internet phenomenon where influencers capture the process of opening products with their viewers, sharing that experience on social media. It shows no sign of going anywhere. It has grown in popularity over the past decade and seen millions and millions of viewers checking out what's in the box. The anticipation and reveal generates excitement and can be a massive marketing opportunity for brands.

It's a low-cost way for you to engage with your intended audience and it can get your products in front of audiences that might not otherwise engage with you. Well-designed packaging can create excitement and anticipation during the unboxing process, leading to positive reviews and word of mouth publicity. And it's fun!

Merchandise

Translating your personal brand into a physical product can be achieved successfully through various types of merchandise that you can create to promote your brand's reach. They can serve as marketing tools, promotional materials and even revenue streams.

I use branded mugs when I am recording one of my podcasts. To my masterclasses that I run all over the world, I bring pens made from recycled paper. I love it when people who attend my masterclasses share their experiences of what they are doing to promote their brand. In a masterclass that I hosted in Glasgow, United Kingdom, one attendee came wearing her branded hoodie. She wore it everywhere and found that people would often approach her and say, "I saw your Instagram post." Her branded hoodie became synonymous to her brand and attracted others to her page and to what she was doing.

Your merchandise can also be sold, depending on what your personal brand message is. There are branded accessories like tote bags, phone cases, keychains, or wristbands that can carry your logo or personal branding elements.

As I mentioned in relation to packaging, sustainability is a key consideration when it comes to any physical stationery or collateral. Today's world must see us being both practical and thoughtful. Who needs another memory stick or reusable plastic water bottles? As practical as they are, I have an entire shelf in the kitchen of unused ones. Consider your impact on the planet. When I launched my Styling Academy in 2018, I gifted everyone who attended a small plant, and a note to say thank you for helping grow the next generation of fashion stylists.

Brand credentials

Credentials will anchor your audience; your reputation will make you stand out in your market. This document is sometimes better known as a pitch deck or your digital marketing collateral. It's your one-stop shop to demonstrate projects that you have undertaken in the past, share client testimonials, or even information about your business such as your purpose, values and strengths. It can often be the difference between securing a new client or not, so it's important you get it right before showing it to any potential clients.

TOP TIPS FOR PRODUCING YOUR BRAND CREDENTIALS

Your brand credentials should be a dynamic document that can evolve as your personal brand and business grows and changes. It needs to be kept current with regular updates to reflect your latest achievements so that it remains relevant to your audience.

It's an essential tool for building trust, credibility and understanding between your brand and your target audience. I've found that the key elements are:

- Consistent branding: a consistent look and feel with your visual branding elements, such as logo, colour scheme and typography. Documents should be visually engaging and memorable, with the use of high-quality images and graphics essential.
- Highlight achievements: build credibility and trust by showcasing your personal brand's achievements and milestones, such as awards, certifications, or significant accomplishments.
- Showcase your team: people connect with people, so putting faces to your brand can humanise it. Introduce key members of your team, their expertise, and their roles within your organisation if you have one.
- Feature testimonials and case studies: share client testimonials and success stories to demonstrate the value and quality of your products or services. They will form powerful credentials.

Media kit/speaker profile

The easier you make a journalist's life the more likely you are to secure a feature in a publication, whether that's a glossy magazine, newspaper or an online article. Your media kit should include an easily accessible biography, stats sharing your social media following (bearing in mind that nano influencers can make more of an impact than those with big followings) and high-quality photography that can be downloaded.

Podcast cover

Whilst you may not be considering developing this medium, it is worth bearing in mind that it will provide you with an instant community and the medium of podcasting allows you to build intimacy with your audience. When you set up your podcast, you will need a visually appealing and well-designed cover to create that all important positive first impression and to encourage people to click through to and learn more about your podcast. Podcasting can serve you well in terms of establishing and reinforcing your personal brand and building consistency. It also signals professionalism when you take your podcasting seriously and are committed to providing valuable content to your listeners. A consistent cover design helps with long-term recognition, making it easier for your existing listeners to find any new episodes and content, while helping new listeners see just how much content you've produced at a glance.

What is Stationery and Why it Matters

Slide presentation

How many of you have heard the saying "death by PowerPoint"? It's never a great way for your personal brand to be remembered. But when all your collateral is in sync and each piece speaks to the others, a well-delivered, succinct PowerPoint or keynote presentation enhances your personal brand.

Branding elements such as colours and imagery can evoke emotions and connect with your audience on a deeper level. An emotional connection between you and your audience can strengthen the impact of your messaging. The ability to showcase your unique identity means your audience is more likely to remember your content and brand after any presentation you deliver, thus increasing the chances of future engagement.

I use the Mac version of keynote for my presentations, because they are specifically designed to appeal to my variable audiences. That said, I always check to make sure that the presentation is compatible with devices in situ or that I can screen share from my technology. Sailing by the seat of your pants is never an option when a slide presentation is part of your key delivery.

I was at a recent event where one of the key speakers experienced her worst nightmare. She had, in fact, been ill prepared, and not done her pre mic and presentation check. When her slides loaded, the fonts made no sense at all. Whilst she tried to brush off her faux pas in a very light-hearted manner, the damage was done, her personal brand was massively affected and the engagement from the audience was poor.

A well-branded presentation exudes professionalism and is the very essence of deseeding the lemon, because it's all about attention to detail. It illustrates that you take your content and messaging seriously.

Newsletters

Having an on-brand newsletter that you can consistently share weekly, bi-weekly or even monthly keeps your personal brand and business at the top of potential clients' inboxes. Digital marketing expert Jenna Kutcher, who is also an author and the podcast host of **Goal Digger**, recently commented how email marketing has acquired 40 times more customers for her business than Facebook and X (formerly Twitter) combined, and yet it is so very often overlooked.[11]

After sending hundreds of emails over the years, I have learned the best ones to engage readers are short, authentic and actionable. Think value, add a visual element (we love gifs at the moment), make sure the title is catchy (often ours has an emoji) and be consistent. For some that might be by sending your newsletter on the same day every week; for us it's making sure we engage with our audience twice a month. Don't forget to include one

---

11 Kutcher, J. (2019) *What you really need to know about starting an email list.* https://jennakutcherblog.com/email101/.

CTA (call to action) and a PS is often the most looked at section in the newsletter.

Lead magnet/quiz

A personal branded lead magnet or quiz can be a powerful tool when growing your online presence, building your email list and nurturing relationships with your audience. The key to making these effective lead generation tools is to offer valuable content or insights to interest your target audience. They can act to entice your audience to provide their contact information, such as email addresses, in exchange for access to the content or quiz results.

A well-designed lead magnet or quiz that provides valuable insights or solutions positions you as an authority in your field. It demonstrates your knowledge and expertise, helping to build trust with your audience. You can drive audience engagement through your PowerPoint presentations or shared QR codes, enabling you to gather valuable data about potential clients' preferences, interests, or pain points. I use this methodology often as part of my brand strategy as data we collect can be tailored to our content, products and marketing tactics to better serve our audience's needs.

Engaging quizzes have the potential to go viral on social media and other platforms too. It's a fact that when people find a quiz enjoyable or enlightening, they are more likely to share it with their friends and followers, expanding your reach organically. Your well-crafted lead magnet can be the first step in a lead nurturing process. By delivering valuable content or insights, you can build a relationship with your leads and gradually guide them towards becoming customers or clients.

If you're just starting out with building your personal brand, it's important not to feel overwhelmed. You are not going to need all these tools to add to your tool kit right now. Just be cognisant that you will need to keep building. Remember the metaphor that your personal brand is like a long-term savings account, you can add when it's appropriate and right for you, but just be consistent. Your goal is to establish and reinforce your personal brand identity, by showcasing your expertise, unique style and personality. In doing so, you make yourself more memorable to your audience.

How to start building your personal brand tool kit

Strong personal brands incorporate multiple tools. I've found that a good place to start is to take a look at your digital presence. First things first – just like Jessica from **Harper's Bazaar, Arabia** – is to develop your personal brand website.

I launched my very first website in 2000, a friend who I had met in my repping days in Fuerteventura designed it for me. I was quick to see how I could use it to position myself to my target audience at that time, television. Applying for a presenting job I was able to attach my website link. I stood out and it got me interviews. Your personal brand website is your shop window, your avatar in the digital world. It will demonstrate that you take your personal brand seriously and are committed to building a strong online identity.

It provides a central hub for all your online activities. You can link to your social media profiles, share your latest work, and direct potential employers or collaborators to one place for all the information they need.

Your website is a long-term asset that can grow with you, as mine has over the years, and you can update it as your personal brand evolves and as you achieve more in your career or personal life.

KEY PIP TAKEAWAYS

MAKE THAT DOMAIN NAME PURCHASE FOR YOURSELF OR ON BEHALF OF YOUR CHILDREN:

They often don't cost very much and you never know when you might find the right moment to enact them.

What is Stationery and Why it Matters

START WITH THE ESSENTIALS, OFTEN NO MORE THAN THREE TO FOUR:

The essentials are a website, a professional email signature, a biography and high-resolution photography. As your personal brand grows, gradually expand your collateral toolkit to include items like newsletters, merchandise and lead magnets.

CREATE A PERSONALLY BRANDED LEAD MAGNET AND/OR QUIZ TO BUILD AN EMAIL LIST AND USE IT AS AN EFFECTIVE TOOL FOR GROWING YOUR ONLINE PRESENCE.

Chapter 9:

STRIKE A POSE

Today's world is fast-paced and visually driven, and a strong personal brand has become an essential component if you want to give yourself the competitive edge. Personal branding will let you control your online image and give you the valuable opportunity to provide your audience with transparency about who you are.

Personal branding encompasses a multitude of components. Two aspects that have played a pivotal role in shaping and enhancing not only my own personal brand identity and equity, but also that of my clients are photography and brand guidelines.

Both are closely linked from a visual consistency perspective, which is why they come under Stationery. Brand guidelines define the visual elements that represent your brand, including the use of specific colours, fonts, logos and imagery. Photography used in collateral, such as brochures, websites or social media posts, must adhere to these guidelines to maintain a consistent and recognisable brand image.

Whilst brand guidelines outline the personality and values of your brand, photography choices should align with this brand identity. For example, a brand aiming for a youthful and vibrant image would select photos that reflect these qualities, while a more serious and corporate brand would choose imagery that complements that identity.

I always prefer bright, light clean photography and always of high quality. My choice always aligns with my additional collateral including graphics on social media. I would like this visual representation to be mirrored when you meet me too.

Photography has been instrumental in growing my personal brand. In the last 20 years in business, I have been featured on more than 10 front covers, hundreds of articles on and offline, many of which have included the use of my own high-quality imagery. My goal and your goal should always be to make the journalist's life easy. But it wasn't always like this, and it was a lesson I learned all too well when I launched my personal shopping and styling agency.

I can remember vividly the first time that I was asked to send an image of me to feature in a publication. They asked for a high-resolution image, and I confess in my naivety all those years ago that I had to Google "high-resolution", a term used to describe the sharpness and clarity of an image taken with a quality camera. High-resolution images are a must for print, because otherwise they can become blurry and distorted – not what you want!

I've always been keen on photography, and although far from good, I loved capturing holiday snaps. I headed to my holiday drawer and unearthed my Fuji camera, oblivious to the fact that it was not of the spec required to produce high enough resolution pictures worthy of a magazine feature. Hastily clearing out space on the SD card of my last staff ticket trip to Hawaii, I headed downstairs to the reception area of the building I was living in at the time in Dubai.

I knew that a selfie wasn't going to fit the bill, so I approached the security guard on duty. Fortunately, on this particular day the on-duty security guard was the one who knew me and always said hello. Giving him my brief, I asked if he would be able to take a couple of quick pictures. Somewhat unorthodox I know, but a picture was needed and needed quickly for the journalist.

As the required photograph needed to be high-quality, I decided that it would be better taken in natural light. We headed off to the green expanse on the side of Sheik Zayed Road, a 12-lane highway, in the blazing midday heat. As I sweated my butt off it did occur to me that it was perhaps not the wisest idea and there had to be a better way. I hadn't at the time considered quality either, and sadly this was very much lacking. Neither the camera nor the security guard had the professional edge. Little did I know at this precise moment that I had failed to deseed the lemon!

Heading back to my apartment I downloaded the image and sent it to the journalist. A two-hour exercise. I think you will know the response by return. Whilst I had understood the brief to provide pictures, I had failed to provide professional images.

Quite honestly, I had never really given thought to the production required when celebrities, models or famous figures showcase their digital presence. I had disastrously missed the point as to how crucial it was to prioritise the quality of images to appeal to my potential audience. I booked my first ever photoshoot. Today I still make this investment on a regular basis. High-quality images convey professionalism and show you care about how you are presented to the world.

I've lost count of how many photoshoots I have invested in. It's a medium that will help to establish your credibility enabling you to easily visually communicate your personality, values and expertise. High-quality and professional photographs demonstrate your competence and show that you take your personal brand seriously, positioning you as an authority in your field.

Without a bank of images, you can't create a beautiful website, share your content on social media, create marketing materials, or be featured in publications, so when I say it can significantly elevate your personal brand's overall perception, I really mean it.

Practice is the key to success. Having learned from the errors of my ways, journalists now get an array of full-length, half-body, landscape and portrait options which they can use to suit the layout of their article.

Photography: a solid investment

Although I have lived in Dubai for over 20 years, my hometown is Edinburgh, Scotland. As a Scottish girl living overseas since I was 18 years old, I am always flattered when I catch the eye of a local publication. One such newspaper approached me to feature in their fashion publication after they saw I had been nominated in the category Scottish Communicator of the Year, in the Scottish Fashion Awards to be held in London.

The then-annual event had, to date, been hosted around Scottish castles and museums and this was the first time the Scottish Fashion Awards had invaded London. Founded by Dr Tessa Hartmann to celebrate leading Scottish fashion talent, fashion names vying for the coveted awards included the likes of Jonathan Saunders, Christopher Kane, Louise Gray and Holly Fulton – all of whom are now incredibly well-known Scottish designers in the fashion world. Among the awards up for grabs were Scottish Designer, Scottish Creative Excellent, Scottish Young Designer, International Designer, and the category that I had been nominated in, Scottish Communicator.

As a shortlisted nominee, the Edinburgh publication was keen to run an article about me and asked for a high-resolution image. I was ready this time and had deseeded the lemon. I was able to package the perfect picture and much to my mum's delight she picked up the local newspaper and found that I was sharing a page with Andy Murray, our famous Scottish tennis player. Even better, my image was centre page and much bigger than Andy's – sorry Andy for grabbing your limelight on this occasion!

While spending money on quality and expensive photoshoots might have been seen as an extravagant or non-essential investment in my early days, this article proved that it paid off; half page cover, on the second page – not too shabby.

As I have grown my social media content pages, I have gone on to work with photographers from all around the world. Capturing behind-the-scenes footage and street-style content became a must as my business and personal brand visibility expanded.

While it can be tempting to do photography "on the cheap", using friends and family, there really is no substitute for someone with a professional eye. Over time I realised that many of my travelling companions, whilst they liked taking photographs, were not that good at capturing moments suitable for social media purposes. They shot from unflattering angles, were too close or too far away, used poor lighting and often over-exposed the pictures. While not every photo needs to be a work of art, there are standards and etiquette that you need to stick to.

A good photo needs to have compelling composition. I have two good amateur photographers in my portfolio – my husband and my mum. Each of them can capture quite unusual pictures that tell a story, or capture an emotion, a particular light or detail and they take more than one shot.

But they are not always with me on my travels. Whilst it requires a financial investment, if you want photography to reflect your story in all manner of locations, always hire a professional photographer.

Sharing your brand with your audience is a valuable way to engage with them. You will always find affordable ways to hire a photographer no matter where you are in the world. You can go online to look for special deals or use your own platform to reach out to your audience and ask if they know anyone that might be keen to step in to help you. I used this approach recently for my engagement party that I held in a hotel in Edinburgh. I wanted to capture the moment and found a new photographer who was just starting out, who offered us a great package and produced amazing "in the moment" photos on the day.

As my visibility increased and my brand reached further worldwide, I have hired photographers in Los Angeles, London, Barcelona and the Maldives. I have changed outfits in the back of cars, behind bushes and sneaked into hotels. I've been photographed on the ledges of high-rise hotels in Dubai, nearly floated off the lip of an infinity pool in Thailand and posed on top of a helipad. I have photos of me taking afternoon tea with the giraffes in Nairobi and the outback in the desert. The more creative the better because this bolsters your social media stories. It's one area that I advocate passionately with my clients as I support their personal brand journey; capture your moments.

As you build your personal brand, events, masterclasses and workshops are all opportunities to capture what you do to share with your viewers. Laura Laugier is one of my clients. She coaches parents who have children with special needs. A parent herself with a child who has a rare chromosome disorder, Cri du chat syndrome that affects 1 in 35,000 live births, Laura has found herself struggling, many times, without support networks as she navigated parenthood.

Creating her personal brand strategy, we knew that she had to maximise her impact from the outset. The importance of capturing content was not lost on her. Laura's first speaking event was to be her platform to raise awareness of who she was and her story – it was the perfect opportunity to capture the visual content we needed. Laura received a fee for speaking at the event which she ploughed back into her business, hiring a photographer to put together an introductory video and photography of her in action. This meant that our creative team at Brand YOU Creators could add this to her website, which we had been designing.

A picture says a thousand words

Great quality photographs create an emotional connection and increase audience engagement. Inherently all humans are visual beings, and strong visuals have the power to evoke emotions and forge connections.

As part of brand strategy, Brand YOU Creators develop photography and brand guidelines for our clients. Adopting this philosophy will allow you to curate your own visual narrative to elicit the desired emotional response from your audience. When you consistently use imagery that reflects your personal brand's essence and values, you foster an emotional connection with your audience, leading to increased engagement, loyalty and a stronger personal brand overall.

My photography bank contains thousands of images, which include press-style photoshoots. Some are taken in a professional studio, great for websites and marketing collateral, others are better suited to lifestyle content, because they have a more behind-the-scenes feel or document a real-time experience.

TOP TIPS FOR A SUCCESSFUL PHOTOSHOOT

For you to get the best results from your personal brand photography session, I would encourage you to maximise the experience and make a list of your goals for the photoshoot.

- What are your considerations; are you rebranding your website, launching a new product or service, or do you need to elevate your personal brand on social media?
- Where are you planning to utilise your photographs? Are they for your company website or for marketing materials?
- Do you need a headshot to position yourself on a speaking panel or on your social media, something that might accompany a thought leadership article for example?

Photography for your website should always have a mix of portrait and landscape shots, so make sure you give a clear brief to your photographer.

Do your homework – hiring a good photographer means you need to take time to study their skills as well. Your photographer will be responsible for representing you through imagery, so make sure they are a great fit for your personal brand. Check their style of work, how creative they are, whether they capture the detail you require and what their storyboard is like.

For the past ten years I have worked with Shyrell Tamayo, founder of MillionWays. I found her after I had seen other business owners' images and asked who they had been using. I confess to a little stalking to make sure Shyrell was the right fit for me. She was, and still is, my go-to, my creative source and the one with a great eye for detail, content and creativity.

Shyrell has taken photography that adorns book covers, appears in adverts on social media and features in countless pieces of marketing collateral; not only for me, but for my Middle Eastern clients too. Her trademark white, light airy style, with sophisticated seating arrangements, shelved and minimal office setups, has created the personal backdrop for timeless and contemporary personal branding shots.

Projecting the right image

Create a mood board for inspiration to help you visually achieve the right look for your personal brand. Subtle body language can convey distant or defensive messages. Avoid stances with the classic arms crossed, for instance. Vanessa Van Edwards' book Cues shares an experiment she conducted with her friend and online marketing expert Brian Dean.

Vanessa saw his website; it headlined a photograph of him with his arms crossed. She suggested replacing it with an alternative pose, one with uncrossed arms. She stated, "It will make you look more open minded and make people more open to opt in to get your email updates."

Strike a Pose

Brian agreed, but he wanted to see if this really was true, so he tried a split test on his website, where 50 per cent of visitors saw the image with the open arm pose and the other 50 per cent saw the crossed arms picture.

The result, over a period of 90 days, was that 237,797 people accessed Brian's website with the open arms posture increasing website conversations by 5.4 per cent.

You should always consider a cultural context. Where possible your photography and guidelines should embrace diversity and inclusivity to a broader audience. Use your visuals to avoid stereotypes and tokenism, and promote your genuine and authentic self to engage with people of different ethnicities, genders, ages, abilities and body types.

Deseed the lemon; create your own lookbook for personal styles and outfit inspiration you like, colour palettes that resonate with your brand and props that can convey your message.

Plan your outfits in advance, try them on and take your own mirror pictures in them. What you wear can make or break your personal brand. Your personal style communicates to your audience who you are, what you stand for and your message – it's so essential that it's Slice Two. Think about how you want to be perceived and consider how to follow your brand colours within your photos. For example, if you have neutral tones for your website, you won't want to be wearing a red dress in your photos as it will clash with the overall vibe you are trying to portray.

When it comes to the shoot itself, you should take a minimum of four looks with you. Start with your least favourite look, as the first set is where you will warm up and get more comfortable posing in front of the camera. You may want to consider taking a formal, semi-formal and casual look to show all sides of your personality. I tend to adopt the following formula for my own photoshoots look: a playful suit, a couple of dresses and a blazer, shirt, and jeans combination.

Don't overlook the use of accessories to help further your message – statement shoes, striking earrings, or a hair band can all deliver a different look. Choose items that are you, this way you will attract people who like you for your vibe. Kai Simmonds, one of my clients who is a soul purpose and burnout coach, really embraces bold colours in her branding and her wardrobe choices reflect her high-energy, dynamic style. She's pictured wearing everything from burnt orange suits to purple slip dresses and pretty statement accessories.

Practise your posing. This is probably the one aspect that makes my clients feel the most uncomfortable, but with just a little pre-practise it can help you feel more confident during your shoot. Explore your favourite angles, favourite side, hand placement on hip, slightly touching an earring, hands held in pocket (remember to leave a thumb out), crossed legs and so on. Work out what poses you feel comfortable in, while being mindful of how these come across to your audience.

Think of the triangle rule, it's a game changer. When posing you want to make triangle shapes with your arms and with your body – it's more flattering because it can make your arms look slimmer and lengthens your legs. It's more natural too, so you look less awkward, and you have something to do with your hands.

Observe your facial expressions and try different ways to smile; lips closed, lips slightly apart then try a full "Kelly smile" which is mouth open and smile as if you really mean it. Vary your poses by looking at the camera and just slightly above and to the right or left of the camera. There's a link to a video about posing for photoshoots in the Resources section at the end of this book.

Say YES!

Say YES! I do a huge amount of professional speaking and have found it quite challenging to get great images when I am delivering my talks. I'm often caught mid-flow, with my mouth usually making a very strange shape. It just looks weird. I found that the best way to overcome this was to stand on stage pre-event, look as though I am speaking to my audience and say YES. By saying this simple word, it gives great shape, looks engaging and can be mixed in alongside real-time images, just in case your photographer hasn't quite captured you in your best moment.

Hire a hair and make-up artist too. Find out if this is included in your photography package, if not make sure you book one prior to the day. I personally love doing my own make-up, but I do always find when a professional make-up artist does it for me that the photos from the shoot just look much more flawless and the make-up stays where it should be for the duration of the photoshoot.

There are all kinds of prop ideas that you can use – a laptop, fresh flowers, food, coffee table books, magazines, your favourite mug, book, notebook, or pen, candles, cue cards, sports equipment and even pets, children, or friends (who can act as clients in group situations). And don't forget any product placement of your own branding.

Once you have all your outfits picked and props organised, put together a shot list. This should include all the images you want your photographer to capture. An example could look like this.

- Laptop in cream suit
- Holding marketing collateral in suit
- Podcast mic landscape and portrait
- Relaxed seating in dress
- Favourite mug relaxed outfit jeans

Not every website or thought leadership piece will require your profile picture, although from personal experience when a photo is included performance is enhanced.

Other types of images to use

In some circumstances, you may want to use stock images rather than photos from a bespoke photoshoot. Stock images, created by photographers that are available for use by others, can often be offered for free. Some though may require a subscription or royalty fee. They can serve as a useful addition for you to use on your website or in marketing collateral. You can choose from a wide range of subjects, styles and concepts, making them a convenient choice when you need visuals that you can't capture yourself, either because you don't have the time or the budget to produce a similar set up on your own.

It's important you choose the visual style, colour palette and tone of any stock images you use to ensure they align with your brand's identity, creating a consistent and recognisable look. Never pass stock images off as your own photos. Your own images need to be unique and genuine, capturing real moments, products, or experiences specific to your brand or personal life.

It can be good practice to use a combination of both till you build your own library, with stock images filling gaps when you need diverse or specialised visuals. When you do use them though, just make sure they offer a true representation of your identity.

Know your brand identity

Combine your photography with clear visual brand identity guidelines, your assets such as logo, colours and fonts that you are going to use throughout your personal brand will serve as a framework that ensures consistency and recognition in how your personal brand is presented across different platforms and mediums.

When Brand YOU Creators create personal brand visual guidelines for our clients, they outline specific rules regarding logo usage – including size restrictions and how your logo should be displayed on different background colours – typography with the different typefaces and families, font sizes and the hierarchy of the fonts your brand uses specified, plus colour schemes that complement each other using RGB and CMYK colour codes, to ensure your personal brand colours stay consistent between web and print versions.

Consistency breeds familiarity and builds trust, both of which are essential in cultivating a loyal following. In addition, having clear guidelines elevates your personal brand's professionalism. It demonstrates that you take your personal brand seriously and are committed to presenting yourself in a polished and coherent manner, plus it saves time as you don't have to constantly reinvent or second-guess how you present yourself.

Deseed the lemon – the extra effort it takes at this stage will, in the long run, save you time and allow you to focus more on creating valuable content and engaging with your audience. Guidelines can also include your core message, values and goals. They define the essence of your personal brand and help you communicate effectively with your target audience. If you collaborate with other individuals or brands, having clear guidelines can also help align your brand with theirs, creating a harmonious and impactful partnership.

By leveraging the power of consistency, professionalism, differentiation, emotional connection and adaptability, you can establish a compelling personal brand that resonates with your audience and sets you apart from the competition. Embrace the potential of brand guidelines and photography to bring your personal brand to life and leave a lasting impression on those who encounter it.

KEY PIP TAKEAWAYS

INVEST IN A PROFESSIONAL PHOTOGRAPHER:

Build your bank of high-quality images that reflect your personal brand. This should include a minimum of five landscape and five portrait photos, all of which have been updated in the last 12 months.

CREATE AN INSPIRATIONAL MOOD BOARD:

Include personal styles, outfit ideas and props that align with your brand's essence and values.

CREATE PERSONAL BRAND GUIDELINES:

Develop a clear visual brand and define your guidelines. Describe the tone and style of communication you want to maintain across all platforms, as well as logo usage, typography, colour schemes and font sizes. Differentiate yourself from others and emphasise your USP.

SLICE FOUR:

SOCIAL

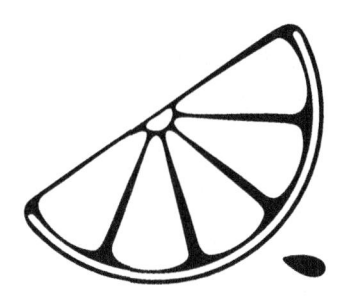

Your social media and digital presence buys you recognition in the mind of your potential or existing audience, whether they're consciously consuming or casually browsing. It's an essential component of personal branding. How you elevate your credibility and visibility requires a thoughtful and detailed strategy; it requires you to thoughtfully deseed the lemon.

Social media refers specifically to online platforms and applications that allow you to create, share and interact with your audience by sharing content. Amongst the current platforms you have access to are Facebook, Instagram, X, LinkedIn, YouTube, TikTok, Pinterest and Threads, all of which focus on real-time interactions, content sharing and community building. That list is not exhaustive.

Your digital presence, on the other hand, encompasses a much broader concept online that extends beyond social media and embodies all touchpoints through which and in which you can be discovered and engage with your audience. It refers to your overall online visibility and reputation, which includes your website, blogs, portfolio, articles or publications, guest appearances on podcasts or webinars, and more. Of course, social media is a very important part of this digital presence.

The social media space continues to evolve and what's hot today might not be tomorrow. Big hypes can fizzle out fast. How many of you can remember the excitement around the introduction of Periscope and Clubhouse during the pandemic? These platforms were a flash in the pan, which

Slice Four: Social

is why it's important to be mindful of where you focus your energy when it comes to posting on social media.

Social media offers you a platform as one of the easiest and fastest ways to establish yourself as an innovator and trailblazer, an expert in your profession. There are countless books and articles available either in bookstores for you to buy or read online about how to grow your social media following. This book is not one of those. Instead, consider this slice as if you were to take a bird's eye view of how to create your personal brand strategy to actively promote your social media presence.

In this slice, I'll offer advice about how to choose the right social media platform to boost your online presence and make meaningful connections with your audience, as well as share how you can create content that builds connections without all of the stress.

Chapter 10:

HOW SOCIAL ARE YOU?

The adage "quality over quantity" holds true when it comes to your social media presence. Being active on numerous platforms can quickly become overwhelming and lead to a diluted impact. It's not about posting everywhere and hoping for the best. It's far more effective to invest your time and effort into a select few platforms where you can truly shine. What algorithm works today on Instagram can flop on TikTok the next.

The goal is to find the sweet spot for a social media platform that's right for you. The right strategic approach that's focused on your interests and targets your audience can be far more effective and maximise your impact. What is obvious to you can be amazing to others. You need to be tenacious in your pursuit to build your reach and be seen as a thought leader in your niche.

Which platform(s) should you use?

As opinions go, mine is that one of the most important elements of personal brand presence on social media is to focus on what you enjoy, and choose platforms that align with your interests and passions. Select platforms that genuinely resonate with you as each platform has its own unique style, purpose and content formats. By selecting platforms this way, you are more likely to be motivated to create engaging and authentic content. When you enjoy what you do, the evidence will be projected in your posts, improving your connection with your audience.

A post you make live on your social media feed that you think is amazing and well-designed to engage with your followers may well be perceived as unimportant or lacklustre once it's out in the world. And vice versa – an insignificant post in your eyes may very well excel with engagement. Often how a post performs comes down to its honesty, realness and the time of day that you share it. No matter how obvious, what I have learned is not to overthink the outcome or the level of reach. It's important to keep trying. Some posts that I have spent lots of time and energy on really don't perform well, and others that I have edited quickly and "in the moment" perform incredibly well.

Different social media platforms attract different demographics. The interests and user behaviours vary significantly from platform to platform. The key to successful social media outreach is to research and analyse which platforms align with your intended audience. This can be achieved by identifying and understanding your target audience. Consider their age group, preferences and online habits. You need to know who these people are and where they hang out. By focusing on platforms where your audience is already present, you increase the likelihood of reaching and engaging with them effectively.

One question I get asked a lot is "Do I need to be on every single social platform?" I think it can be incredibly challenging to spread yourself on every social media platform. The daily demands of everyday life make this not only time consuming, but also physically and mentally draining, especially if you don't have a team behind you. When I work with my clients, we take time to establish what their primary and secondary platforms will be at the outset of any brand strategy. It's key to their social media success.

For instance, my primary social media platform is Instagram. It's the place that I enjoy the most for sharing both professional and personal life stories. It's where I have my biggest following. Even if your primary platform receives most of your attention, you need a backup, a secondary platform that allows you to expand your reach. I find that LinkedIn is a close second for me.

I've been actively using Instagram since 2009 (a long time!). It's part of my active personal brand strategy; all my clients are using it, either contributing to their own accounts or following others. It's where I make a lot of connections, many of which result not only in increased exposure, but also in gaining new clients who are looking for a personal brand strategist.

When you are deciding what your primary and secondary platforms are going to be, it's important to evaluate the platform which has the highest concentration of your target audience. Are they seen to be more active on Instagram and LinkedIn, like me, or are they to be found through Facebook, X, Pinterest, or a niche platform specific to your industry or interests?

Consider the type of content you enjoy creating and what format suits it best. If you're a visual storyteller, Instagram or Pinterest might be an ideal platform for your purposes. If your preference is written content, platforms like LinkedIn or X can prove to be great options.

Actively assess the growth potential of a platform too. Is it still gaining traction, or has it reached its peak? Being an early adopter of a platform with upward momentum can give you a competitive advantage. Threads, for example, saw many people attract a huge number of followers quickly when it first came out in 2023.

Consider the location in which you find your ideal clients too. Both cities and countries can have their own trends for social media and communication. I remember being in Los Angeles in October 2016 and being really surprised to find that hardly anybody there used WhatsApp as a messaging app, despite it being introduced around 2009 and being incredibly popular elsewhere. By contrast, in the Middle East an extraordinarily high amount of business is now conducted on WhatsApp. Meanwhile, instant communication tools like Snapchat are popular in Saudi Arabia for building personal branding; whilst in China the preference seems to be WeChat or Weibo, largely because many Western social media sites are banned in the country.

Your secondary platform should always compliment your primary one. For example, if your primary platform is YouTube, using X or Facebook to promote your videos can help increase viewership and engagement.

My third platform is YouTube and I repurpose a lot of my Instagram reels into YouTube shorts. Your second and third platforms should enable you to connect with influencers or industry experts who might not be present on your primary platform, because this will help broaden your network and, theoretically, enable you to tap into new opportunities.

Using platforms where you can repurpose or adapt your primary platform content to fit their format allows you to save time while still catering to a different audience.

When you know where your future clients or prospects are, define your personal brand voice and values. Your language and messaging should align with your expertise and target audience. This will provide a consistent foundation for all your social media communications. What's your tone? Informal, to the point, casual or data driven and informative? How do you describe yourself? Uplifting, amusing, fun, or witty?

One big company brand that I find particularly fresh is the digital bank Monzo. They are a great example of "tone and voice". They start by saying: "We're ambitious, positive and always focused on what matters to people." Their voice is witty and light-hearted, sprinkling, as they say, a little magic dust. Works for me! They are so far removed from a serious and dry tone that you might associate with banking.

What should you post?

Once you have identified your platforms, target audience and tone of voice, you want to create content pillars as part of your personal brand social media strategy. Content pillars are three to five topics your personal brand will consistently discuss, amplify and create content for on social media. They can also be called content categories or content buckets. Whatever you call them, these topics form the foundation of what you'll post and really help you stay focused and make planning so much easier. How do you choose your content pillars? They need to align with your business goals: what do you want your audience to do after seeing your content or how do you want them to feel?

Example of my content pillars:

- Personal branding and business tips (educational or inspirational).
- Relationships (husband, family, friends, all of whom are very important to me).
- Fitness (inspiring/unintentionally educational).
- Lifestyle (behind the scenes, skincare, holidays, and influencer experiences).
- Podcasting (educational, inspiring).

Once you have determined your pillars, explore the endless possibilities of how to curate your own content that's a mix of educational, inspirational, funny (if that's your vibe), or engaging behind the scenes that showcases you as relatable and positions your thought leadership. Incorporating a variety of formats into your posts, like text, images, videos, and infographics, will go a long way to keeping your content diverse and appealing.

I actively encourage my clients to repurpose content. There is an art to achieving effective repurposing without your content feeling repetitive, but the key is simple: link it to one of your content pillars. I remind my clients to reflect before they do and remember that each platform has its own tone and style, and not to repost the same message across all their channels.

When I was invited to dine at Nobu in Atlantis the Palm, Dubai, I adopted the same approach. Nobu has been on my husband's bucket list for a while. This experience was a great fit for one of my pillars – lifestyle. On occasions such as this I compile behind-the-scenes themed content of what I do on a weekend and use those images on my primary and secondary social media platforms – each with different messaging. On my primary platform, Instagram, I shared a carousel of ten images. Creative culinary plates of food, a light-hearted picture of me trying to eat with chopsticks, somewhat unsuccessfully, and a picture of me and my husband with the Head Chef Damien Duviau.

For my secondary platform, LinkedIn, I used only one of those images, the picture taken with the Head Chef Damien Duviau. The intention was to share with my followers Nobu's absolute perfection of the presentation, the quality of the dining experience and the talent of his team. The cuisine exceeded our every expectation. Nobu, in their very own unique way, deseeded the lemon.

The authentic, genuine and well-crafted narrative saw my posts on both mediums perform unbelievably well. Many of my audience, and those who I am connected to on LinkedIn, commented on their experiences at Nobu too, or intimated that they would be following in my footsteps to join Chef Damien Duviau and his team for a fine dining experience. Giving credit where credit is due, and shining the light on others' expertise, cultivates strong positive emotions which are uplifting and energising.

In my role as brand strategist, I frequently hear clients, and those in business working alongside me saying, "I don't know what to say in a post." I have lost count of the number of times I have heard this or been told of the fruitless hours they have sat staring at a blank screen waiting for inspiration to make its grand entrance.

As an avid reader, you will often find me with my nose in a book (usually the latest business or personal development title), or searching the internet for interesting blogs and podcasts from like-minded entrepreneurs. This was how I came across Jasmine Star, former photographer, now world-class speaker and business strategist, who mentors entrepreneurs and has been strategizing businesses across the world. In one of her podcasts, she shared her formula that she and her team use to curate and post content. She calls it her HIC Formula which stands for:

- **HOOK:**
  Have a scroll-stopping headline that captivates your audience.

- **INSIGHTS:**
  Value that you're offering to your audience.

- **CALL TO ACTION (CTA):**
  Boost engagement by asking your audience to do something.[12]

Star's philosophy as to why her formula works so well is because it begins with a hook, in her words "a caption to entice your audience to read more." She believes that when someone scrolls through your feed, you want to be sure that what you write at the beginning is in fact so captivating that it stops their scroll. Try it yourself. I can tell you from personal experience it works!

---

12 Star, J. (2021) *The Easiest Way to Post On Social Media - Jasmine Star.* https://jasminestar.com/easiest-way-to-post/.

How Social Are You?

Kelly Lundberg · You
☆ Personal Brand Strategist | Business Mentor | TEDx Spea...
2w · 🌐

This is where you can find me 👀

With a remote team, I've never needed to have extra space for calls & meetings but my needs have changed & this year have a dedicated sound proof booth for my calls & office space.

The bonus.....

It's right next to the gym I go too... 💪

I always thought I was more productive WFH but I think I may have been missing out. There is no fridge to raid, washing to do & any other tidying distractions 😅

Are you more productive in the office or WFH? Let me know below 👇

#personalbrand #uplevel #wfh #kellylundberg

Mary Rose Chambers and 123 others   20 comments

203

> **Kelly Lundberg** · You
> ☆ Personal Brand Strategist | Business Mentor | TEDx Spea...
> 5d · 🌐
>
> Want to know what it takes to scale multiple 7 figure businesses? 🎙️
>
> Lisa Johnson recently stopped by Dubai and shared her insights on growing and scaling multiple 7-figure businesses. From personal brand building to industry insights, Lisa shared honest tips and mistakes to avoid in your journey towards success.
>
> Stay tuned for this episode, where Lisa's wisdom and expertise will be on full display. Thank you, Lisa, for being so generous with your time while you were in the sandpit 🌴. We can't wait to learn from you!

How to achieve content consistency

There is no definitive answer to how often you need to post in a week. Planning, consistency and frequency are central to keeping not only your audience, but also your platform algorithm engaged. Determine the optimal frequency for each platform you propose to use, and create a content calendar to plan and organise your posts. Navigating the ranking signals on each platform to get your content seen takes experience. Algorithms on every social media platform are different and will change all the time.

For example, on Instagram I am currently posting ten times per week, while on LinkedIn I post four to five times per week. You don't need to hit those numbers, just know that these platforms reward consistency.

When planning, keep what you are trying to achieve at the forefront of your mind. Think about who you are trying to reach, how you will measure your success, how often you will post and what time you will post at. If you define your goals and metrics at the outset, it will help you to tailor your content and ensure your strategy is specific to each platform you have chosen as your preferred social media method of communication.

Many people make the mistake and overcommit by saying they are going to post five times a week, when they don't have the habits or routine in place to even post once a week. Scheduling content can be a game changer. Knowing that you have a few posts already collated that can be timetabled over a period of time helps with the consistency of being more visible. Combining some of your scheduled posts with real-time, behind-the-scenes content will help keep your personal brand authentic and current. It's a winning strategy. I find it quite comical that people automatically assume you are doing well the more visible you are. Perceptions will always vary.

To make the best use of my time when it comes to content creation, I will set aside time once a month and map out what type of content I want to share, write my scripts and create a list of style examples that I want to recreate for my personal brand. This is my time to deseed the lemon, the extra attention to detail in the planning process sets me up for success and will do the same for you, setting you apart from others.

I then book out a further hour another day, either to spend with a professional photographer or, if you feel confident enough, by yourself with your selfie stand, to record content. If you are planning to self-edit, best practice is to complete it all in the same day, while your thoughts and intent are fresh. Many of my clients when they first work with me share quite honestly that they are spending far more than an hour every day thinking about what to say, creating content and then posting.

If you are one of these overthinkers, doing this five times a week means you are spending at least 20 hours a month on content creation. How sustainable is that? The formula that works for me is to first plan, which usually takes around one to two hours. I then schedule a time to record and edit, usually around three to five hours, which can vary depending on how much content is being created. Finally I schedule another one to two hours to schedule all the content I have created. Even if I take my upper estimate, it comes to nine hours per month – that's a saving of more than half. If you can squeeze your budget and it allows some bigger spend, check out Fiverr for local freelance talent to do edits for you, releasing even more hours to explore and focus on other elements to build your personal brand.

Remember it's a conversation

Actively engage with your audience by responding to comments and messages. By doing so you can foster conversations, answer questions and provide valuable insights. The interaction you have builds belief, strengthens your personal brand and creates a community around your expertise. I find it can be a useful strategy to go back to your previous posts, answer all the comments and engage with those who have liked it. When you have just posted a new piece of content, engagement on your previous post will drive more people to your current one.

Regularly monitoring and analysing your social media performance is overlooked by many. However, it's surprisingly easy to do using the analytics tools provided by the platforms or third-party applications. Assess metrics like engagement, reach and conversions to understand what content resonates with your audience. Use these insights to refine your strategy and optimise your social media presence. It's the small details that make the big difference – your turn to deseed the lemon.

Personal branding beyond social media requires you to integrate your social media presence with your overall personal branding efforts. For your personal brand to impact your opportunities in your career, business, relationships and in real life it must extend beyond what you say on social media.

Keep it consistent

All touchpoints, including your website, should have consistency. It's a word I say a lot. If you want to do better things and experience personal progress, consistency is a must-have skill for success. It instils discipline, sharpens attention and increases awareness about what needs to be done.

I've lost count of the number of times that I have checked clients' existing websites only to find they have a broken link, otherwise known as dead links or link rots. On the surface you might be thinking that a broken link is not so bad, but the truth is that it can do some serious damage to your reputation and personal brand, not to mention damage to your website.

What happens when you access a website and a dead link appears? You may get a 404 error page, "link not found" or "sorry page not found". When this happens to you, I bet you hit the back button to exit the site. If this was your website it could potentially mean a lost customer and loss of revenue.

Blogs, speaking engagements and offline interactions make it easy for people to tag you into posts. Create a cohesive personal brand that extends beyond social media to establish a strong and recognisable presence.

Be yourself

Being authentic on social media is about being genuine, honest and true to yourself. Authenticity builds stronger connections with your audience, fosters trust and creates a positive online presence. Many people find this aspect of personal brand building the hardest due to fear of judgement or rejection, imposter syndrome or all-round self-doubt. I always like to remind my clients that what is obvious to them is amazing to others. You only need to be one chapter ahead to share some knowledge, no matter how big or small, to help or inspire someone.

All it takes is for one person who sees your post to feel it resonates with them and to do something or show up differently as a result for that post to have had a positive impact. When you come out of your own head space and think about it, what you do can really help someone. When helping others, what you share is no longer about you. That's a great space to be in.

When I decided to include fitness as one of my personal brand content pillars, I began a journey. I had no idea where the journey would take me other than I knew that hitting my late 30s I wanted to have a healthier and fitter lifestyle, a better balance. Along my journey there have been good days, challenging days, fun days and days that were not so much fun and I didn't want to show up to the gym, but I did and I documented it. Even today, although I am four years-plus along my fitness journey, it still surprises me the amount of people who message and say that seeing me at the gym inspires them to get up and go too. I even revisited my first fitness post alongside a more current one and posted that too. What can you do to inspire someone else? You just never know who is checking out your social media pages.

Share your successes and failures and be open about your experiences. Your authenticity on social media should be quite simply who you are. No airs or graces, yet so many people find it challenging to translate this into their content. The key is to know what your values and purpose are, what you stand for and what message you want to convey – this is why considering these things is part of Slice One: Strategy. Share content that aligns with your values and reflects your true self. Be real and honest rather than portraying a false or overly curated image of yourself.

Whilst it may seem obvious to engage with your audience, respond to comments, messages and questions from your followers, taking the time to engage with new profiles shows appreciation. Remember social media is meant to be social, it's not just a platform for you to post content, hoping that people will find you or that you might go viral.

Share personal stories, anecdotes and experiences that have shaped you and can help your audience relate to you on a deeper level. Sharing your passions, things that genuinely excite you, is contagious and can draw people to your profile. Admit your mistakes and learn from them, acknowledge and demonstrate what you've learned from the experience.

Another top tip is to avoid over-filtering. While filters and editing can enhance your photos, be cautious not to overdo it, as it may create an unrealistic portrayal of yourself. Years ago, I attended an event hosted by someone I'd been following on social media for quite some time. I then met her in real life and had to do a double take. This couldn't possibly be the same person I was following on social media with her flawless skin and perfect features. As it turned out, she was far from being real and genuine on her social media profile and this did not resonate with my personal brand values. The person I'd been following was not who I met; I won't name names, but I unfollowed her.

Do I ever use a filter? Yes, I do on occasion, usually on stories when I'm posting about early morning trips to the gym around 4–5am or when there is poor lighting. The odd filter does not make me unreal; I am truly comfortable in my own skin. I am me and I live and breathe being my personal brand. My point is that there is a difference between using the occasional filter and filtering every photo you post to the point that someone who follows you on social media wouldn't recognise you if they passed you in the street.

Whatever your preferred level of social interaction is, extrovert or introvert, your pitch on social media may vary. If your personality style is that of an introvert, you may find you are less comfortable posting your profile on social media platforms. You do, however, need to post both personally and professionally to establish and grow your personal brand.

Whilst nothing beats the power of a visual and personal representation, there are ways where you can effectively navigate the process and make it feel more manageable. Focus on creating high-quality, meaningful content that resonates with your audience. Reliable posting, albeit less frequently, where you share thoughtful content can still prove to be more effective than posting frequently with random updates.

Leverage your strengths – you may find that you excel at creating in-depth and insightful content, which LinkedIn loves. Build connections, and don't be afraid to engage in conversations with your followers. Used to its advantage the sharing of valuable information, personal stories, or expertise will be helpful and appealing to others.

Carefully crafted personal brand guidelines, with uniform graphic elements, give you a strong visual identity. Your brand guidelines should represent, with absolute clarity, your brand's personality and values to maintain a consistent and recognisable brand across your content.

What if you don't want to always be front and centre?

Not comfortable with using your profile? Invest in high-quality images and graphics that align with your brand and message. One of my clients who was working in the corporate arena was not able to use her profile to promote her side hustle. Her employer was unaware that she was looking to make personal career changes. I suggested that she create an avatar that represented her brand. You could use an illustration or a cartoon version of yourself or a unique character that embodies your personality. Another thought would be to use stock photos, illustrations, or commissioned artwork that resonates with your target audience. Be wary with this option as mentioned earlier in Chapter 9, as you can start to lose some of your authenticity if your alternative profiling is too generic.

Share content from other creators who align with your brand's values and themes. You can curate articles, quotes, infographics, or videos that resonate with your audience without necessarily showing your profile.

Consider creating audio content such as podcasts or voice recordings. Your voice can convey your personality, knowledge and validity, providing a great opportunity to further strengthen your personal brand. I love sharing behind-the-scenes content, where you can offer glimpses of your work process, projects, or daily life without being front facing directly. This can create a sense of authenticity and connection with your audience.

I have some clients in Saudi Arabia where culturally women are typically expected to cover their hair and sometimes even their faces in public. They have found creative ways to build strong social accounts by sharing behind-the-scenes content – such as from coffee shops, shots of the accessories they are wearing, their latest handbags and one of the women I work with has even shown off her collection of cars now she is able to drive.

Gather social proof

Encourage your audience or clients to share testimonials or reviews about your work or products; make it easy for them to share their thoughts. Use a link on your website, incorporate testimonials into your workflow or include a request for testimonials as part of your client off-boarding process. Make it standard practice to ask for feedback at the end of your working relationship. Positive feedback from others can strengthen your personal brand's credibility and reputation.

The key thread throughout when actively building your personal brand on social media is to focus on demonstrating your expertise and knowledge in your field. Share valuable insights, tips and tutorials that showcase your skills and position you as a thought leader in your niche.

KEY PIP TAKEAWAYS

IDENTIFY YOUR STRATEGIC APPROACH:

Rather than chasing trends on different social media platforms, choose a select few that align with your interests and target audience. Quality over quantity!

CHARACTERISE YOUR TARGET AUDIENCE:

Research and analyse which platforms attract your intended audience. Effectively tailor your content to resonate with them.

ALIGN WITH YOUR INTERESTS:

Select social media platforms that genuinely resonate with you and where you can create engaging and authentic content. Passion and enjoyment will shine through in your posts.

PLAN AND SCHEDULE CONTENT:

Create a content calendar to plan and organise your posts. Schedule content in advance to maintain consistency and efficiency.

BE AUTHENTIC AND TRUE TO YOURSELF:

Share personal stories, insights and experiences. Engage with your audience genuinely, respond to comments and messages, and be open about your journey. Authenticity builds trust and stronger connections with your audience.

Chapter 11:

HIREBARBARA.COM

As social media continues to evolve, keeping abreast of platform algorithm changes, new policies and best practices, can be overwhelming as you continue building your personal brand. It can, however, be inspiring and encouraging to learn what has worked for others and consider how you can implement a strategy to work for you.

With that in mind, I'd like to introduce you to Barbara Oseicka, a client of mine. She used her personal brand and the power to leverage herself on LinkedIn with extraordinary results. Barbara quite unexpectedly lost her job and spent several months applying for roles without success. Disillusioned and feeling battered and bruised by constant rejections and a lack of responses to her many applications, during one of our sessions I suggested that we look more creatively at her personal brand strategy to ensure that she could stand out from the crowd and really deseed the lemon. In her case all her competitors were also seeking a new job. Our plan was a simple one: create a CV that would make her noticeably different in her niche – learning and development.

Step one was to showcase and capture the attention that her skills and experience deserved. We needed an eye-catching headline – meet hirebarbara.com! Barbara had already designed a website for her coaching business using Wix.com, so I knew she could create a professional-looking website for her personal brand. I suggested that she share her expertise by downloading her CV to her new site hirebarbara.com, the objective being that anyone interested in her skills and expertise could reach out and contact her directly.

Step two of our personal brand strategy was for Barbara to create an authentic video, which she shot organically at her home. Making this into a suitably sized reel she was able to attach it to a post on her social media platform. Her post on Linkedin went like this.

Deseed The Lemon

Over three months ago, I lost my job.

This entire time, I've been applying for the jobs however I was mostly receiving thank you emails. Everyone who was looking for a job at least once knows how tedious and discouraging the whole process can be.

If you were waiting for a plot twist, I am sorry to disappoint you. This is not one of the success stories... yet!

There is a quote I like "If the plan doesn't work, change the plan, but never the goal." Since my current plan hasn't worked for me so far, I made a new one.

I created a website:

hirebarbara.com

to present my achievements and valuable qualities I bring to the table which can be missed if you only look at the traditional CV.

Great things are achieved together therefore I would like to ask my network here on LinkedIn if you could please like, comment, and/or share this post to spread the word. 😊

And if you are an employer looking for a creative employee like me please get in touch.

Because it would be amazing if my next post would be about a SUCCESS STORY! 🤞

Please note I'm looking for roles in Dubai.

Step three, Barbara attached this reel to her social media platform, pressed the button and sent it out into the world. Her post went viral! On day five I got a voice note saying, "I think we broke LinkedIn." Her post had reached over 4.6 million views with job opportunities coming in abundance, not to mention the occasional marriage proposal.

Over the period of the next two weeks, she replied to everyone (yes everyone) with a personal note to thank everyone who had taken the time to reply to her. She deseeded the lemon. No small feat. Her post was even seen by someone in Australia, who told a friend of theirs in Dubai to look at it. She had countless Zoom meetings with people all over the world with exciting and unexpected job offerings, finally landing a role which she loves.

Why did our strategy work? Her post was genuine and authentic. She applied the principles of the HIC formula, Jasmine Star's philosophy, that I shared in Chapter 10. There was a clear call to action. Asking for help, something many people are afraid to do, can have results way beyond your wildest dreams. By getting vulnerable it allowed Barbara to stay in Dubai, where she had firmly put down roots, bought a home and had a network of respected friends. She didn't want to leave and was prepared to do everything she possibly could to stay there. I am so proud of her resolve and drive to succeed.

Working with like-minded, hungry and focus-driven individuals, my clients are all action orientated. I find that when we have taken time to create a personal brand strategy, they very often go the extra mile and get the results – as evidenced by Barbara.

Why LinkedIn?

LinkedIn as a social media networking platform has advanced significantly over the last few years. It operates in a totally different way to other social networking sites. That said, that's not to say that in time other competitors won't step into the marketplace and challenge LinkedIn's prominence in the professional social media space. Although it's not the largest social network, for now LinkedIn remains a firm favourite in the eyes of many as an amazing platform to connect, expand professional networks and grow your personal brand presence.

Specifically designed with networking in mind, LinkedIn offers you the opportunity to connect with people you already know or have been introduced to by someone in your network. It's a platform for professional and industry-related content, providing an environment for you to share your expertise, insights and thought leadership content in a context that is directly relevant to your industry or niche.

LinkedIn's algorithm tends to favour organic reach for valuable content, which means your posts have the potential to reach a broader audience without the need for extensive advertising. This can help your personal brand gain visibility and traction.

As a closed network it has less noise and clutter, making it easier for your content to stand out and gain attention. It has become the leading platform for building a network of relevant connections and expanding your professional reach. You can keep your network fresh and active, and strengthen your global connections whilst validating and credibly building trust, as well as helping to position you as an authority and thought leader in your field.

When it comes to reputation and credibility, LinkedIn provides opportunities to showcase your professional achievements, education, skills and endorsements. By creating a compelling LinkedIn profile written in the first person, and regularly updating your profile with recommendations and relevant content, you can build a strong reputation and credibility within your industry. It serves not only as an online CV, but as a portfolio that can impress potential clients, employers and future collaborators.

There is the option to publish long-form articles directly along with the ability to share in-depth insights, industry analysis and thought-provoking content to a wide professional audience. Publishing on LinkedIn all contributes to establishing yourself as an expert, gaining visibility, and attracting engagement and followers. The great thing about LinkedIn is that it doesn't require constant engagement or day-to-day management to perform well for you.

LinkedIn is no longer just a platform for individuals to search for jobs, employers can actively search for potential candidates, and professionals can seek new job opportunities. By maintaining an updated LinkedIn profile and actively engaging with the platform, you increase your chances of being discovered by not only recruiters, but also by potential clients who may be interested in your skills and expertise.

Collaborate to grow your personal brand

Leveraging social media to collaborate with other thought leaders, influencers and professionals in your industry is another great way to increase your visibility. If you choose to engage in meaningful discussions, share each other's content and participate in joint initiatives you will expand your reach and network.

In 2022, one of my clients used this personal brand strategy so effectively it grew her LinkedIn account by 534 per cent in 12 months resulting in a 40 per cent increase in sales. Lucy Bradley, founder of Plug Communications, a successful marketing agency based in Dubai, approached me to work with her on her personal brand strategy. She already had her design and execution in the bag. However, her personal brand audit identified that she had less than clear goals, which were holding her back. Our strategy was to launch a personal brand website, elevate her personal style to suit her personality and create a social media strategy, something that Lucy appeared to be a little lukewarm on.

Lucy, as I and others who know her are well aware, loves to meet people. She is very engaging and is a prolific networker. Despite loving networking in person, when it came to social media she was struggling to work out what and when to post, how to engage and what platform would work best for her.

An artful communicator and given her love of networking, I knew with a clear strategy Lucy would really grow her personal brand with LinkedIn. For every engagement she had with her clients, industry professionals or thought leaders I charged her to take a picture with that person and share a personal story. I encouraged her to share stories about why she chose to do business with them or what made them stand out to her. It depersonalised the moment, no longer making it all about Lucy, instead making it all about the people she was meeting and the impact they had.

Sharing post after post, these in turn got reshared, tagged and retagged. Only recently, Lucy shared with her somewhat large email list that Plug Communications would be leaving the social media platform Instagram, to focus on LinkedIn. Whilst Lucy does continue to post personally on her personal brand Instagram page about her journey, Plug Communications is concentrating on the LinkedIn platform. It confirms that not only has she the eye to pick a platform that works for her business, but she stays true to her values and very effectively deseeds the lemon.

Shout about your passions

When you stay true to your values and post content that you are passionate about, it attracts the right audience. An attendee of one of my personal brand masterclasses actioned the strategies she learned from me. This particular lady had a fairly inactive Instagram account. She was super passionate about horses, but felt that she couldn't share this kind of content as it didn't relate to her current industry expertise. With increased confidence gained from the masterclass and with clear intent, she began to increase her posts related to her passion. The result?

She received a very surprising enquiry from a freighting company who specialised in relocating horses worldwide. They had a job of interest for her. This just goes to show the power of social media; of course, she made an unexpected job change.

This isn't the only time this kind of thing has happened. During a corporate masterclass about building a personal brand in business, an attendee expressed some reticence that he couldn't share elements of his fitness journey which he was incredibly enthusiastic about. I disagreed, citing that regardless of his thinking, training for a fitness-related activity requires discipline. It demonstrates a committed person, one who values health and wellbeing, and the importance of creating a positive brand image. One of the benefits of having an interest outside business is that you can offer diverse content that is interesting to your audience and potentially reach an even wider audience that are not connected to you in just a business sense.

This happened to me back in 2019, when one of my YouTube videos went viral. It began with a chicken, yes, I kid you not. Intrigued by all aspects of branding and the marketing of brands, I watch adverts from all over the world online. This particular advert caught my eye, it was from the brand known as Jollibee (the Filipino equivalent to McDonald's).

Jollibee created a series of adverts that really pulled on the heart strings, with their ethos very much about appreciating moments and finding ultimate joy. The advert I had stumbled upon was "Vow & Perfect Pairs". Keen to establish an emotional connection with my audience about feelings and thoughts, I filmed myself viewing the advert and a few others of theirs.

I became immersed in the moment – I laughed and cried watching these adverts, my reaction was honest and genuine. It has also resulted in a combined pull of millions of views which, still to this day, generates revenue for me from YouTube. It's a great example of diverse content, delivered authentically, attracting increased viewership from an expanded audience.

Dress up your shop window

Treat your social media platforms like your shop window. They serve as a public display that showcases your personal brand, products (if you have them) and services to the world. As with a shop window, social media provides a glimpse into what you and/or your business has to offer and entices potential customers to step inside (visit your website or send a connection/follow request) to explore further.

Just as a shop window creates the first impression of a physical store, your social media profile is often the first point of contact for potential customers. It sets the tone for their perception of your brand. The design and layout of a shop window often reflect the store's branding. Similarly, your social media presence helps reinforce your brand identity and personality. A shop window tells a story about what customers can expect inside the store, and social media enables you to tell your brand story and create a narrative around what you are all about.

The best part is social media allows you to showcase your brand to a vast audience beyond the geographical limitations of a physical shop window; your personal brand is global. If that's not a reason to step up your social media game, what is?

Remember, while it's essential to try new strategies, it's equally important to track and measure their effectiveness. Deseed the lemon, analysing the data from your social media experiments. If you are willing to make the extra effort, it will help you identify what's working and what isn't, enabling you to refine your social media approach over time for maximum impact.

MY INSTAGRAM EXPERIMENT

Finally, don't obsess over numbers, focus on building meaningful connections rather than obsessing over follower counts and likes. Authenticity will naturally attract the right audience. It was one of the big reasons I made the decision to leave my original verified Instagram account with 50,000 followers and start all over again in August 2023. Over a ten year period, I had accumulated what the industry describes as bots or dead accounts. I didn't resonate with my account any more and wanted to stay true to my values and share content with people who could see it and benefit from it. I also wanted to confirm all the strategies that I share with my clients, who are often just starting out, really do work!

> The strategy, at the time of writing this book, worked! I was very aware that not all my following would move over to my new page, and in the first seven days I accumulated just short of 1,000 followers. Over the next four weeks that doubled, and the account continues to grow. In this time, I had reached over 40,182 accounts and had over 200,000 Impressions with just four per cent of my original following – this was more than I had achieved in the previous four weeks with 50,000 followers. I went on to launch my Brand YOU Accelerator Program, sharing it on my new account with around 2,000 followers with no paid ads. This resulted in a $14,000 product launch.
>
> Followers I hadn't connected with in years became much more visible now, rather than being lost in the noise. Some people messaged me saying they wanted to do the same thing I had, as their account didn't resonate with their personal brand any more. Some told me I was brave. I'd say I took a risk, yes, but brave? No. What was the worst that could happen? I could always go back, but to me, continuing to do the same thing I always had, and getting little or no visibility, just didn't make sense anymore.

Social media is an embryonic landscape, and businesses that stay open to experimentation and adaptation are more likely to thrive in this dynamic environment. Every audience is unique, and what works for one business or personal brand may not work for another. Trying new strategies allows you to understand and leverage these algorithm changes to improve your reach and engagement, plus trying different strategies enables you to diversify your content.

KEY PIP TAKEAWAYS

INVEST TIME IN A LINKEDIN STRATEGY:

Recognise the potential of LinkedIn as a platform to build your personal brand. Allocate time to create a thoughtful and well-defined strategy that aligns with your goals and target audience.

EXPERIMENT WITH DIFFERENT STRATEGIES:

Actively track the results, as algorithms are constantly evolving.

KEEP YOUR SOCIAL MEDIA PRESENCE FRESH AND ENGAGING:

Prevent your audience from getting bored with repetitive content.

Hirebarbara.com

SHARE EXPERTISE AND THOUGHT LEADERSHIP:

Leverage LinkedIn's professional environment, and showcase your industry-specific expertise and thought leadership. Share your valuable insights and content establishing you as an authority in your field.

COLLABORATE AND NETWORK:

Engage with other thought leaders, influencers and professionals in your industry. Collaborate on meaningful discussions, share each other's content and participate in joint initiatives to expand your reach and network.

Deseed The Lemon

SLICE FIVE:

SPOTLIGHT

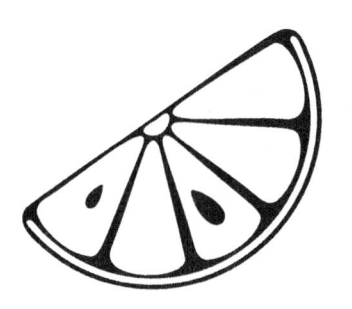

Media coverage plays a pivotal role in establishing and enhancing personal brand credibility for several reasons. Firstly, media coverage provides third-party validation and endorsement, lending credibility and trustworthiness to one's brand. When reputable media outlets feature or mention an individual, it serves as a stamp of approval that can significantly boost their perceived expertise and authority in their respective field. Many people massively underestimate the power of being in the spotlight and this is the focus of the next slice.

Being in the spotlight elevates your visibility in both the online and offline worlds. The more often you are captured on and offline, the more people will have the perception that you are doing well in business. They will also become more familiar with your personal brand, making it easier for them to find you, recognise you and engage with your content on social media. Exposure in the media space very often leads to the expansion of your network. It gives you the valuable medium to connect with influencers, thought leaders and collaborators, which can enhance your reputation and social media presence through strategic partnerships and collaborations.

In the next two chapters, I'll give you an overview of how to start reaching out to the press to build your profile, and talk about collaborations, strategic partnerships and how you can make them work for you and your brand.

Chapter 12:

FROM AIR HOSTESS TO AUTHOR

It was a chance conversation with a friend in the very early days before I had even launched my business in the summer of 2005. My friend, and fellow cabin crew colleague, Vanessa and I had just spent three days together on an Emirates crew trip to Jakarta, Indonesia. I shared with her my idea and my plans to set up a personal styling business in Dubai, StyleMeDivine.

As I animatedly shared all my plans, she told me that as part of my strategy to launch the business I would need media support to get my business out to an audience. Talk about bursting my bubble! Vanessa said I would need to consider preparing a press release and to target the biggest media outlets I could find. It all sounded very fancy and official, and I had no idea what a press release looked like.

My internet research revealed that a press release was an official statement delivered to members of the news media for the purpose of providing information, creating an official statement, or making an announcement directed for public release. Sounds simple, well the theory of it did. According to Wikipedia, press releases are also considered a primary source, meaning they are original sources for information.

Post our Jakarta trip, I sat down to write a press release to send to the media, with support from Vanessa, who had marketing experience from her life before taking to the skies, and armed with what I had learned with my Google research. With the press release finalised, all I needed to do next was find out who the best contacts were to send it to.

Low on budget, but ever resourceful, I took myself off to a bookshop in Dubai. It was an easy way to look up the glossies which were stacked high in the newspaper and magazine section, alongside books. Those were the days long before the internet and LinkedIn made everything easier. Leafing through as many fashion magazines as I could, as well as local newspapers, I copied down as many contact names at Dubai's publishing houses along with landline numbers as I could find. Remember this was also in the days before the mass use of mobiles and WhatsApp.

Swiftly exiting before I was asked to make a purchase of said magazines, I made my way home to make the calls. I had targeted 20 print publications and my mission was to find out who the editor was of each of them, successfully soliciting their email addresses. Having found out who to contact, I set about emailing each with my press release. The effort to deseed the lemon paid off!

Within the first eight weeks of launching my business and sending out my press release, I achieved no less than six features in print publications, one of which was Dubai's **Ahlan Hot 100** where I had gained a top spread in the section as **"One to Watch"**. The **Hot 100** was a list of Dubai's movers and shakers, the ones who dared to dream. It featured many of Dubai's top entrepreneurs, philanthropists, style icons and personalities who were shaping the emirate's landscape.

The **Ahlan Hot 100** was, at the time, an annual coffee table publication of who's who, everyone who was anybody wanted to feature in this hotly contested, highly coveted publication. Through this notoriety, I got my first paying press work with a local newspaper **7Days**, who ran a feature on shopping and styling trends in Dubai. They hired me as a stylist to curate content that was focused around "shop the look for less". I would, once a month, curate four different looks sourced from local boutiques, high-street stores or designers, which would be photographed and put into print for their weekly fashion segment – think celebrity runway looks, but sourced for less.

This was all the proof I needed to confirm that media coverage widens the reach and exposure of a personal brand. Being featured in newspapers, magazines, TV shows, podcasts, or online platforms exposes an individual to a broader audience, expanding their visibility and attracting new followers, clients, or opportunities. I achieved publication success in my hometown of Edinburgh too. In 2011, the **Daily Record** ran an article "Scots personal shopper on dressing big spenders in Dubai's capital of bling". Some articles can portray you in a more favourable light than others, but they all served to increase my visibility that not only enhanced my credibility, but also created a sense of relevance and importance in the eyes of others. It's an absolute must when it comes to a Google search of who you are – this is all part of boosting your overall digital footprint.

Media coverage will serve to differentiate you from your competitors, so it's an essential component of building your personal brand. We are all too aware of occupying a saturated market. Being featured in the media sets you apart, establishing a unique selling point and creating a memorable impression. It adds a layer of distinction and professionalism to your personal brand, elevating it above the noise and making it more desirable to potential collaborators, clients, or employers. Now it's your turn to shine the spotlight on yourself and deseed the lemon!

How to get noticed by the media

One key aspect you must consider is that media outlets tend to favour personal stories and human-interest pieces rather than just business facts, as stories tend to resonate more with audiences on an emotional level. Media outlets understand that stories about individuals, their struggles, achievements, or unique experiences will capture the attention and empathy of readers or viewers.

We are naturally drawn to narratives that evoke emotions; personal stories have compelling content. If you are someone who shies away from the limelight it could hold you back as you look to build out your personal brand. Personal stories have the power to connect with a wide range of people. By featuring individuals, media outlets know they are showcasing real-life examples, anecdotes and personal journeys that others can relate to. This relatability helps engage and resonate with audiences, fostering a sense of connection and empathy. The future of business is personal.

I experienced this first hand in 2009, after I published my first book **Success in the City, Dubai Entrepreneurs Tell Their Story**. Grazia Middle East approached me to feature me in one of their upcoming publications. **Success In The City** was a collection of stories from 20 entrepreneurs who had launched businesses, all within Dubai, and become trailblazers within their niche.

I was inspired by stories I heard from those around me, particularly after attending an awards ceremony for SMEs in Dubai held by Lloyds TSB Banking Group, where I learned about many amazing small businesses. One of my first research stories was about Swedish entrepreneur and philanthropist Thomas Lundgren, who was also Founder of THE One, a furniture retail company. Lundgren battled to get funding for his startup business, approaching six major banks in the Middle East only to be dismissed as not a viable business option. He hung those six rejection letters on the wall of his first office, to inspire his employees and show them anything was truly possible. His home-grown family business has gone from strength to strength. THE One now has a total of 27 stores and one bistro restaurant across the Middle East and North Africa. No doubt by the time you read this he has added yet more. Not bad for this philanthropist with a vision to "save the world from IKEA".[13]

During the launch process of **Success in the City**, when interviewed by a journalist for a local magazine I made it very clear that the book was not about me. It was all about inspiring business owners, who had touched me with their stories, visions and the strength of their personal brands.

It's typical though in the publishing industry that you don't get to read the article till it's printed. On the day of release, I headed back to the very same bookshop where, just a few years earlier, I had spent hours copying the names and numbers of publishing houses, and picked up the latest copy of **Grazia**. Adrenalin pumping, anticipation at an all-time high, I opened the double-page spread and cringed "Air Hostess to Author" – not quite the title I had expected and it certainly did not fit with the personal brand image I wanted to create.

As I tried to absorb the content of the article all I could think was, what will people think of me? My initial take was it smacked of "look at me", once an air hostess and now an author. It made me feel uncomfortable. For starters, air hostess is not a term we use nowadays in the industry. Closing the magazine I left the shop without purchasing a copy. I felt uncomfortable with the exposure I had received and felt that the journalist had failed at every point to

---

13   Anil Bhoyrul, (2015), 'Thomas Lundgren doesn't like IKEA. Can you blame him?', *Arabian Business*, 3 May, available at: https://www.arabianbusiness.com/industries/retail/thomas-lundgren-doesn-t-like-ikea-can-you-blame-him-591192

capture the essence of my book and the message I was looking to share with others.

Like many of my clients when we first start together, I hadn't appreciated the power of personalising and humanising businesses. The journalist was right to focus on me as a person. While my intention was to promote the individuals and businesses featured in my book, I realised the driving force behind the project was my personal brand and my story added depth and authenticity to the narrative, making it more relatable and resonant with the audience.

While featuring businesses themselves is essential for certain topics, incorporating personal stories within business coverage can humanise the company and the person and make it more relatable. By highlighting the individuals behind each business, along with their motivations, challenges, or successes, the media can add depth and human connection to the narrative.

The penny finally dropped; it was one of those aha moments – people inherently connect with people. Whether it's in the world of advertising, branding, or publishing, the realisation struck that the most powerful way to engage and resonate with an audience is through personal connection, and I needed to make those personal connections in the same way. I had helped the entrepreneurs behind the businesses featured in **Success in the City** share their stories, now it was my turn.

Individuals are drawn to stories, personalities and relatable experiences, and by humanising your messaging, and by sharing authentic stories and voices, you can foster a genuine, emotional bond with your audience.

Leverage LinkedIn to build media connections

The days of sitting in a bookshop are long behind me. I use LinkedIn as my place to connect with individuals in the media these days. It's one place where you are more than likely to get a response. During the summer of 2016 I spent time in Los Angeles, as I felt this was the right place to grow my celebrity styling career. One of my goals was to be on **E!** in the fashion segment. I also wanted to have conversations on the red carpet and see what that might lead to. Upgrading my LinkedIn membership to Premium enabled me to search and reach more people, including many I had otherwise not been aware of. LinkedIn's Premium membership also allows you to send lots more InMail messages than the free version.

I was delighted when I connected to the producer of the show which led to initial meetings. Unfortunately, time ran out before it could gain any momentum, as I had to return to the Middle East. It was confirmation, however, that if you just get clear on who you want to connect with, it can be easy to start to develop relationships. It is even easier today with so many choices of social media platforms.

Use PR experts to boost your profile

As my business and personal brand grew, I knew there were significant benefits to PR. However, building and managing a personal brand's PR efforts can be time-consuming and resource intensive as you grow bigger. By hiring a PR company, you can delegate these responsibilities to professionals so that they can help deseed the lemon for you, allowing you to focus on other aspects of your brand or career.

PR agencies have the necessary infrastructure, tools and networks to streamline PR activities, saving you valuable time and resources while achieving optimal results. I first started working with Tash Hatherall, publicist and founder of TishTash Communications, a London and UAE-based public relations and marketing agency, ten years ago and she's since gone on to become one of my closest friends.

We initially met on the red carpet of a fashion awards show, where I was working on behalf of Yahoo!, interviewing everyone attending on the red carpet. Tash and her team were the PR team for the event who were handling all the celebrity talent, managing interviews and the guest list. We immediately clicked and met up after the event to discuss working together.

There are so many advantages of working with an agency, especially one like TishTash Communications, as they possess a deep understanding of media landscapes, audience targeting and effective communication techniques. By hiring a PR company, you gain access to their expertise, industry knowledge and established relationships with media outlets and influencers. They can navigate the complexities of public relations on your behalf, maximising your personal brand's exposure and impact.

They have also established excellent relationships with journalists, reporters and influencers across various industries. They know how to pitch your story, secure media coverage, and leverage these connections to generate positive publicity for your personal brand. PR professionals, like Tash, can identify media outlets that align with your personal brand image and values, increasing the likelihood of getting featured in relevant publications, TV shows, podcasts, or online platforms. Their expertise in media relations enhances your chances of receiving widespread coverage and exposure.

The key thing about PR, and something to realise as you embark on it, is that results don't just happen and that you get from it what you put in. Don't think you just hand it over to an agency and your part is done. You need to enable it, so work with the team on content and ideas. The people who benefit the most from their PR activities are those who embrace it and who grasp every opportunity. One great example of someone who has really worked the PR game well is mine and Tash's mutual client Christiana Maxion, the dating coach who I introduced in Chapter 4. Full of energy and a desire to put herself out there to achieve all her future goals, Christiana has followed the advice of her PR team, taking on every media opportunity with both hands. Of course, the fact everyone always wants to hear relationship advice helps! In just a year Christiana has been featured over 200 times in the media across the globe and has very much become the go-to expert for all things dating. The more you're seen out there, the more you're asked to do.

You may be at the start of your journey and possibly your budget doesn't allow for hiring a PR company, so below is an example of a press release and what you can include in it.

Press Release
Dubai, 19th January 2022

Kelly Lundberg Launches Brand YOU Creators

Agency Launched to Create Personal Brands for CEO's and Entrepreneurs

Dubai based business mentor, personal style and brand expert, Kelly Lundberg has launched Brand YOU Creators, a specialised agency dedicated to C-Suite executives and entrepreneurs at www.brandyoucreators.com looking to amplify their personal brands and influence ahead of the competition, with expertise from Kelly and the Brand YOU Creators team.

Brand YOU Creators utilises Kelly's highly successful Brand YOU Strategy to simplify the personal branding process in a way that works for the individual, whatever industry space or business stage they are in, and helps them to establish the correct market positioning for themselves to drive traffic, cultivate authority and garner trust from colleagues, clients existing and new, and industry peers alike.

As the concept of 'personal branding' becomes more of a professional need in a modern and agile market, Kelly Lundberg has spent the last three years running

Brand YOU workshops, classes, mentoring sessions and consultancy under her own personal brand. Now having seen businesses launch, sales figures triple, and strong visibility with media presence from the Brand YOU alumni, the time has come for Brand YOU to have its own space. Brand YOU Creators exists to help busy executives and entrepreneurs find the turnkey solution for creating their personal brand with a strong online presence, to position themselves where they want to be.

Kelly Lundberg says; "Whether you're an entrepreneur or an employee, a C-level exec or currently creating a side hustle, your personal brand doesn't just determine what is said about you when you walk out of a room, it's what Google says about you in every room there's a device connected to the internet. It's vital in 2022 that we are able to create the correct professional or creative narrative for anyone that seeks us out"

Brand YOU Creators offers the opportunity to follow a self-paced 25 module online course, enjoy workshops, masterclasses and brand building exercises alongside one to one consultancy and mentoring with Kelly herself. Brand YOU Creators can also build a bespoke suite of digital assets, from websites, to social media content, graphics, stationary and more.

Over a 20 year career, starting in the personal styling industry, Kelly Lundberg has propelled herself to an award-winning business owner, business mentor, and international speaker, garnering an ever growing loyal following across several social media platforms, from which she shares her business knowledge, personal branding and style advice with practical tools for self-empowerment.

Kelly continues; " In a world where our digital identity and our physical presence are increasingly intertwined, brand identity is more important than ever. Our place in the digital world is more important than ever, so it is vital to make it authentic - to align it to your own true values and those of your organisation. What might have previously been a 'nice to have' or even ignored by those more introverted, your online personal brand, via the power of search, is often the first interaction anyone will have with you - potential employees, employers, clients and customers. I'm excited to launch Brand You Creators as a one stop platform that gives individuals the opportunity to show the world their authentic selves, and build their credibility and businesses alongside"

Brand You Creators is now live at www.brandyoucreators.com and on Instagram @brandyoucreators.

– ENDS –

About Brand You Creators:

Brand YOU Creators is a specialized agency dedicated to C-Suite executives and entrepreneurs looking to amplify their personal brands and influence ahead of the competition. Brand YOU was founded by Dubai based business mentor, personal style and brand expert, Kelly Lundberg in 2022 after seeing the need for a specialized agency after three years of running Brand YOU workshops, classes, mentoring sessions and consultancy under her own personal brand. For more information visit www.brandyoucreators.com or keep up with the latest news on Instagram @brandyoucreators.

About Kelly Lundberg:

Kelly Lundberg is one of the most diverse business entrepreneurs to have emerged out of the styling world to date. Gaining notoriety as a celebrity stylist, she has since propelled herself to an Award-winning Business Owner, Business Mentor and International Speaker. Lundberg garners an ever-growing loyal following across several social media platforms, from which she shares her business knowledge, personal branding and style advice with practical tools for self-empowerment. By combining the best in catwalk and commerce, Kelly launched: The S.Academy - mentoring business owners on how to launch & grow their very own profitable business and personal brand. She also has a number of best-selling books under her Hermes belt, plus regularly hosts and presents keynote speeches and motivational sessions across the world on a host of entrepreneurship and style led topics, such as her powerful TEDx Talk entitled 'The Currency of Life'. For more information visit https://kellylundbergofficial.com/ and keep up to date with her latest news at @KellyLundbergOfficial.

For media information, please contact:

WHAT GOES INTO A PRESS RELEASE?

The following are the essential components all good press releases should include.

Header: Begin with a clear and concise headline that grabs attention and summarises the main news or announcement.

Dateline: Include the city and date of the press release.

Introduction/lead paragraph: Write a compelling opening paragraph that provides a concise overview of the news or announcement. This should answer the essential questions of who, what, where, when, why and how, while piquing the reader's interest.

Body: Expand on the details of the news or announcement in subsequent paragraphs. Include relevant information, facts, quotes and any supporting details that provide context and enhance the understanding of the news.

Supporting information: If applicable, include additional details, background information, statistics, research findings, or any other relevant data that supports and strengthens the main message of the press release.

Quotes: Include quotes from key individuals or from you. Quotes should be concise, impactful and provide unique insights or perspectives.

Multimedia assets: Consider including multimedia assets such as high-resolution images, videos, infographics, or audio clips that complement the news. Provide captions or descriptions for each asset and ensure they are easily accessible or downloadable for journalists or media outlets.

Boilerplate: Include a brief paragraph about the company, brand, or individual being featured in the press release. This serves as an introduction to the organisation, or person, and provides background information, including key achievements, areas of expertise, or unique selling points. You can reuse the same boilerplate copy on multiple press releases, and you'll only need to update it to reflect changes in your business as it evolves. Ideally this should be between 300 and 500 words long; 400 words is the sweet spot.

Contact Information: Provide the contact details of the person or representative who can be reached for further information or media inquiries. Include their name, title, organisation, phone number, email address and any relevant social media handles.

Call to Action: Conclude the press release with a clear call to action, such as inviting journalists to schedule interviews, attend events, visit a website for more information, or download additional resources. Encourage media professionals to reach out for further inquiries or to request additional assets.

Support in a crisis

There are moments, personally or professionally, where you could find yourself in the middle of a crisis or negative publicity. Whether it's accidental or intended, this is where PR companies excel at managing and mitigating damage to your personal brand. They possess crisis communication expertise, enabling them to handle sensitive situations, respond effectively to media inquiries and protect your reputation. PR professionals can develop crisis communication strategies, draft statements and guide you through challenging situations, helping to maintain or rebuild trust with your audience. When it goes wrong, your PR team can be the most valuable asset you have expertly guiding you through the situation.

With more than 150 publications under my Hermès belt, many thanks to Tash and her team, I can say confidently that making the effort, deseeding the lemon and considering a strong PR strategy to support your personal brand will pay dividends. Ultimately it will help to differentiate you from your competitors. Good PR adds a layer of distinction and professionalism to your personal brand, elevating you above the noise and making you and your business more desirable to potential collaborators, clients, or employers.

KEY PIP TAKEAWAYS

PERSONAL STORIES ARE IMPORTANT:

Media outlets favour personal stories and human-interest pieces as they resonate more with audiences on an emotional level. Sharing personal journeys, struggles and successes can capture attention and empathy, making content more engaging and relatable. Establish your compelling story – what have you experienced, and what triumphs and challenges can you talk about that the media could be interested in?

BUILD RELATIONSHIPS:

Connect on social media platforms like LinkedIn with journalists. Remember it's like dating – develop the conversation and build the relationship first before you ask for something.

CREDIT SUCCESS WHERE IT'S DUE:

Success in media and PR is a direct reflection of the effort and dedication you invest. You reap the rewards that mirror the commitment and personal brand strategy you sow.

Chapter 13:

THINK BIG PICTURE

Attracting press and being featured in magazines and newspapers is just one way you can raise the profile and credibility of your personal brand. Spotlight features in magazines, newspapers and blogs can also monetise your personal brand. To make this happen effortlessly, I always recommend my clients make sure their press kit is crafted comprehensively.

Journalists need to be able to access information about your personal brand and business easily. You will recall the scramble I had to get ready for the press to publicise me when I was launching my personal styling business. Writing a personal biography, not just a business one, taking high-resolution photos (I am sure you remember the story about my first pictures), and capturing my key achievements in a résumé that showcased my accomplishments all took time. As print publications dwindle, and online has begun its domination, what's the best way to ensure you get noticed?

Pitch your story with consideration. Tailor it precisely to specific media outlets, and target the best forum through which to share your story. When you personalise each pitch, it will go a long way to demonstrate your familiarity with their work and give you the in to explain why your story would be of interest to their audience. Make your proposition value driven and unique. Be compelling. Share three to five articles you could write for them, include one sample and see if they like your writing style. Whilst you might not be paid for this, you can gain exposure which often is valued at more than the payment would be for the article.

Build genuine relationships with media contacts

I have found that one of the best ways to achieve successful press coverage is to treat journalists, reporters, editors and influencers like my clients. I make sure I get to know them and build a relationship with them to learn what they are looking for. By engaging with their content, sharing their articles and commenting thoughtfully on their posts it builds genuine relationships and rapport. This takes time, but this is also where I believe the art of deseeding the lemon will help your personal brand to stand out.

This has worked to my advantage many times, particularly during my fashion days when I attended the many social events held in Dubai. Because I had built relationships with journalists, they would often seek me out as they knew they could rely on me for a quote – it made their jobs easier. But they also wanted to catch up – it's always good to see a friendly face after all. Of course, I also benefited by being featured in their publications, so it was a win-win.

PR isn't all about the print media. It's also important to build relationships with those working in the broadcast media, which includes television and radio outlets. This enables you to look for guest appearances both on television network channels and radio shows. I was often asked to be interviewed on television during my styling days. A segment I always gained great exposure from was my commentary during Oscar Award season when I would share my thoughts on the highs and lows of red-carpet fashion or the not-so-fashionable choices. Recently I was asked to appear on another TV show to talk about personal branding and the presenter became a client of mine.

Media outlets often seek out an expert who can offer commentary, analysis or first-hand experience in a particular topic or industry. Also, by featuring knowledgeable experts, the media outlet also enhances the quality and credibility of its content. Take the time to work out where you can fit into features and how you can engage with readers, listeners or viewers. Everything from a personal heartbreak or a joyful story, to career mentoring or charitable work that you love doing can help you gain media exposure. Remember, what is obvious to you is amazing to others.

Don't forget about online publications

With the rise of the influencer, online publications and blogs can sometimes have a far wider reach than traditional publications or outlets. Identify influential blogs that cater to your target audience and pitch your story or expertise to secure featured articles, guest posts, or interviews. Building a strong digital presence that goes beyond just social media endorses your credibility even more, the back links of where your name becomes associated with publications all helps when it comes to your "you are who Google says you are" profile.

Podcasts are another vast opportunity and have gained significant popularity in recent years as the number of podcasts available has grown exponentially. As of April 2021, there were over two million active podcasts and more than 48 million podcast episodes, according to Hubspot's Podcast Insights.[14] This number continues to rise as more individuals, brands and organisations enter the podcasting space. Reaching out to podcast hosts in your industry or niche and securing guest spots or interviews allows you to share your insights, expertise and personal brand message with a dedicated and engaged audience.

I was beyond delighted when John Lee Dumas, founder and host of **Entrepreneurs on Fire** (an award-winning podcast for inspiring entrepreneurs who are ON FIRE),

---

14 Bump, P. (2022) '38 Podcast Stats That Advertisers Need to Know in 2022,' *Hubspot*, 5 August. https://blog.hubspot.com/marketing/podcast-stats.

invited me to be one of his guests. Here's a guy who knew how to level up his personal brand, having used his podcast to successfully help him to grow his business. He had his aha moment at the age of 32, when he decided to host the first seven-day-per-week podcast interviewing successful entrepreneurs. Whilst in the early days, back in 2012, he faced some resistance getting EOF up and running, any effort he put in back then has more than paid off. He has passed 4,000 episodes, gets over two million listeners per month, with a total of over 150 million over the lifetime of the show, and earns over $250,000 per month in revenue.

I was EOF 793 "Kelly Lundberg; A fashion styler who takes the cake with her opportunity for Fire Nation." Last time I listened to him it's still growing and I am still in awe at the guests he brings on to share their stories.

How can you secure yourself a spot on someone's show? As a podcast host with my own show – The Kelly Lundberg Podcast – I want to make sure that whoever I ask to join me will engage with my audience, so that they come back to me again and again to listen. Interesting stories, a good tone, artful listening and clear articulation make it easy for me to select my guests. I've been privileged to interview many guests, and each of them touch me in a different way leaving lasting impressions of personal and professional success stories and challenges.

One such guest was Sarah Brook, who I met in 2021. Her PA at the time, Annabel Jenner, had followed my social media for many years and it was Annabel who reached out to me, telling me Sarah's story was captivating. The more I heard about who Sarah was, and how she turned a near tragedy to reward, the more I knew I had to share her story with my listeners. Sarah is a dynamic and innovative charity leader and founder of The Sparkle Foundation, which is a UK and Dubai-registered charity and international NGO established in 2015, when Sarah was just 19 years old.

If you thought that was impressive, prior to setting up her charity, Sarah had recovered from a severe brain injury that put her in a coma, and had been held at knife point. Rather than allowing these experiences to knock her back, Sarah channelled them into her unwavering will to succeed and do good – hence setting up The Sparkle Foundation.

Her aim is to improve the lives, education and wellbeing of thousands of vulnerable children in local communities in Malawi, Africa, using an innovative, sustainable model that disrupts the traditional charity sector approach. At the time of writing, her charity has fed over 15,000 children. I could not fail to be impressed by what she has achieved in very challenging circumstances. After we recorded her podcast, I found myself asking whether I wanted to make a difference to a child's life. You bet I did, and I found myself signing up to join her as a volunteer. I went to Malawi in 2022, and left with even more stories to share.

The power of collaboration

Like or loathe the social media influencing industry, there is great power in collaborating with the right social media influencer and it can be an effective PR and personal brand strategy. Seeking out the right influencer takes time and requires action. You want to make sure you engage with influencers who align with your personal brand and can promote either your expertise, products, or services to their followers, generating visibility and credibility.

> ## UNDERSTANDING INFLUENCERS...
>
> A micro-influencer is an influencer with a follower count within the range of 10,000–100,000 followers. Influencers are typically broken down into four main types based on their follower count: Nano-influencers: 1K–10K followers. Micro-influencers: 10K–100K followers. Macro-influencers: 100K–1M followers.
>
> Many brands tend to fixate on the sheer numbers associated with an influencer, but it's paramount to understand the campaign's objectives. Nano-influencers may have more frequent and authentic interactions with their audience, making them highly effective for specific goals. In contrast, macro-influencers can bring extensive reach, but their campaigns often come with substantial costs. It's vital to weigh the pros and cons, align your influencer choice with your specific campaign objectives, and consider the most cost-effective and impactful approach.

As with any business arrangement, always have clear deliverables. Collaborations are another lucrative way to build your personal brand visibility and credibility. Over the years I have been offered many opportunities, some I have chosen to work with and promote, some I have not, as they didn't align with my personal brand values or were products or services I would never use. Influencer partnerships or collaborations on social media platforms can be an exciting addition to your personal brand portfolio, provided they are seen as authentic when you're promoting them to your audience.

One of the first paid partnerships TishTash secured for me was with Miele, a luxury high-end appliance and commercial equipment company. They were launching their ultra-lux Fashion Master Steam Ironing System – their solution for crease-free clothing every time. Miele and TishTash PR were looking for someone who would be able to endorse this new appliance. As a celebrity stylist at the time, they approached me to help with their launch in the Middle East. I had the type of client following that would potentially be interested in the benefits of such a product, who would use it and, therefore, ultimately make a purchase. Believe me when I tell you it really was state of the art, with a very high price point. And yes, the clothes looked beautiful after time on the board.

The FashionMaster was a beast. It was not easily transportable, so it was one of my first posts that I shared that wasn't "professionally" shot by a photographer – just a friend who I directed at home. I remember at the time that the post performed surprisingly well. Looking back, I realise the reason was that it was shot in real time and wasn't perfectly curated, which people like. I shared the benefits and showcased it honestly – it genuinely was an amazing piece of equipment, especially if ironing was not your forte (just like me).

Measure for success

It's easy to get carried away and forget that you still need to track your PR efforts. You need a strategy to assess results. Make sure that you take the time to monitor media coverage of your personal brand – the impact can be measured through website traffic and social media engagement, or business leads generated.

Building PR coverage suitable for your personal brand takes time, consistency and perseverance. Don't underestimate the value of establishing and nurturing relationships with the media. You can deseed the lemon perfectly by taking the time to refine your message and adapt your approach depending on feedback and results.

KEY PIP TAKEAWAYS

DEFINE YOUR BRAND AND OBJECTIVES:

Your identity, values and expertise all add up to unique selling points, which you can use to clearly articulate your personal brand. When you identify your target audience, refine the key messages you wish to share. In doing so, you will be able to determine your PR goals.

DEVELOP YOUR COMPELLING STORY:

Craft a compelling narrative that showcases what makes your personal brand unique. Include what has happened on your journey, covering your experiences, accomplishments, the ups and the downs and insights that can be packaged into newsworthy stories or topics of interest.

CREATE AND DISTRIBUTE THOUGHT LEADERSHIP CONTENT:

Write articles, opinion pieces, or research papers for industry publications, online platforms, or your own blog. Thought leadership content helps position you as an expert and increases your visibility within your field.

JOIN ONLINE FORUMS AND COMMUNITIES:

Engaging in relevant online forums, communities, or discussion boards provides opportunities to establish your expertise and connect with your target audience. Participating in discussions, providing valuable insights and answering questions can generate positive exposure and enhance your personal brand's visibility.

SLICE SIX:

SPEAKING

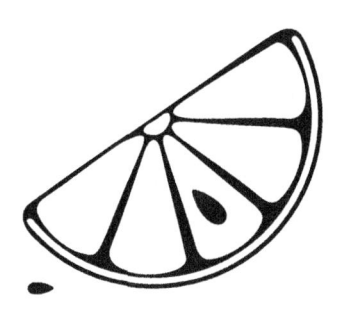

Public speaking allows you to convey your message to a large audience, simultaneously. This efficiency can save time and effort compared to individual conversations with each person. Whether it's presenting to a team, delivering a keynote address, or conducting workshops, public speaking lets you reach multiple people at once.

This saves time compared to engaging in one-on-one conversations, where you would need to invest individual time and effort for each interaction. By addressing a group, you can communicate your message to a larger audience in a shorter amount of time, maximising your efficiency.

I am passionate about helping my clients build their confidence, supporting them with a personal brand strategy that empowers them to host their own masterclasses and workshops. It's those speaking engagements that provide social proof and validation for their personal brand and business. Many of my clients have gone from speaking for free, to a position where they have a product or service to offer which collects leads. Some even now get paid anywhere between $500–$8,000 for a speaking engagement.

When people see you stand up and share something, or hear a compelling presentation, they perceive you as someone worth listening to and following. The fact that you have been invited to speak to a large audience further validates your expertise and personal brand credibility, and you can get paid for this.

Speaking engagements can also provide valuable content that can be repurposed for various social platforms. You can record your presentations, transcribe them, or create

Slice Six: Speaking

summaries to use as blog posts, articles, social media content, or podcast episodes. You can leverage the content from your speaking engagements to reach an even larger audience and establish your expertise across different channels.

Also consider the advantages such as brand association. When you speak in front of an audience, you can associate your personal brand with the event or organisation hosting the speaking engagement. Such an association can boost your brand's perceived value and credibility, as you are aligned with reputable platforms, conferences, or industry events. In short, it serves to enhance your personal brand's image and reputation.

I know that public speaking can be a daunting prospect, but it is crucial if you want to grow your personal brand and elevate your business to new heights. If you're someone who finds the thought of public speaking terrifying, I've got some tips for you to make it feel less scary in the next chapter. I've also dedicated a whole chapter to finding speaking gigs, because once you're confident sharing your message, you need to make sure you get out there.

Chapter 14:

ONE TO MANY

Public speaking is an essential skill to develop when you are looking to cultivate and enhance your personal brand and should be a central part of your branding strategy. Creating and influencing public perception goes way beyond standing on a stage and delivering a speech; it encompasses the ability to effectively communicate, influence others, and leave a lasting impression.

Whether you are pitching to potential clients in a small meeting or in a room full of 500 people with you standing on a stage, public speaking has great personal benefits. Investing in this art builds self-esteem, hones your critical thinking and makes meaningful social connections. You can entertain, engage and educate your listeners. Even better, you have the most wonderful opportunity to inspire.

I have been engaged in professional public speaking since the age of 18 when I delivered "welcome meetings" as a holiday representative in Cyprus. When I say professional, I had no previous experience. I knew that I had to learn this skill quickly if I was to stand out in a teeming marketplace of other holiday representatives, my competitors, all hustling to sell trips and make their commission, which was definitely needed to top up the somewhat meagre overseas wages paid by travel companies.

Those early welcome meetings were far from polished back in the '90s, but they were certainly inventive. I used every tool to my advantage, I even drew a map of the island on the largest piece of cardboard I could find, placed sticky markers for all the local bus stops, using those prompts to tell excited holiday makers what they would find if they explored the island. I would fold it up and carry it from meeting to meeting and replace it again and again when it got tattered and torn. It was all in the detail; little did I know even then I was in fact deseeding the lemon.

Public speaking provided me with a unique opportunity to showcase my personality, passion and authentic self, and I found that I thrived on this and achieved my goal, to stand out from the crowd, connect emotionally with my assembled audience and quickly become one of Direct Holidays' (sadly long since gone bust) top performers. I found it easy to create memorable experiences through my public speaking engagements that helped carve my distinct identity.

But let's take a step back to where and why this all started. I was 18 years old, looking for an escape from the Scottish weather (a common theme) and to try something that was not deskbound and 9 to 5. I think you will remember the Scottish weather has always been a driving factor in my moves overseas. I saw an advert in a local newspaper for an open day for holiday representatives at an Edinburgh-based hotel and went along to find out more.

The open day was well attended and everyone listened intently to the presentation delivered by one of the senior travel consultants. I was sold. This was the perfect job for me. The prerequisites were outlined for applicants to be assessed against and having presented my CV, (yes, I had turned up with a fresh, crisply printed résumé of my working experience, although it amounted to little more than experience gathered since my hair washing days at Dixon Reid), I secured an initial interview and passed to the second stage. It was all going brilliantly, until I was asked how old I was. The job required all applicants to be 21 years and over.

Having just turned 18 I was devastated, but not deterred. There was no way that I was not going to have my second interview. Catching sight of the lady who had delivered her presentation I asked her to reconsider their policy, walking her through my qualifications and experience, in abundance, and the success of my first stage interview. Speaking is often more than just being on a big stage, it can mean the difference of just "speaking up".

I think in hindsight I caught her a little off guard as she reluctantly agreed to allow me to proceed, asking what time the following day I wanted to attend for the interview. I recall saying, "What's the first appointment of the day?

One to Many

I'm always a happy morning person." Little did I know that this statement would work in my favour. Anyone who has been on a package holiday to Europe knows those flights always land at "silly o'clock" in the morning.

I passed the first interview stage of the selection process, gaining a second interview. I was delighted until I read the letter outlining the final stage interview process – I was required to make a ten-minute presentation with the storyline "A Date", the interpretation of the theme being left entirely open. What's more, the presentation was in a public forum with all those selected for final stage interviews. Was I phased? Perhaps just a little, but the role was within my sights.

Creatively some people brought in dates, the fruit kind not their girlfriend or boyfriend, that said that would have been quite original too. Some shared cringe-worthy first date stories. I chose to create a fictional story about winning a date off the back of a pizza box with a Hollywood heart throb – think "Win a Date with Tad Hamilton" only it was five more years before that hit the big screens, maybe someone stole my script! I was armed with homemade props – a pizza box and a wire shopping basket I had persuaded a local newsagent to loan me – all of which went into the mix to make my storytelling more authentic.

Regardless of how silly I may have looked, my presentation and delivery worked. Eight weeks later I was on a plane to start a six-month assignment in Cyprus, and Direct Holidays had just employed their youngest-ever holiday rep.

Little did I know that would be the training to lead me to my TEDx talk some 16 years later. Five days after arrival on the island, I stood up and gave my first presentation about what Cyprus had to offer, shared stories about the wonderful trips, half of which I hadn't even been on but had read about in guidebooks. Was I petrified? Of course.

Public speaking is a skill and I was thrown in at the deep end, but boy did I learn quickly. Over six seasons, I delivered five welcome meetings a week on five different islands. My storytelling and sales got better and better. Public speaking can be terrifying, but even if you are the shyest person, you can start your journey towards becoming a great public speaker. It is a learnable skill and one that if you choose to invest in, pays off in personal branding.

Grow your impact

One of the fastest ways to grow your personal brand credibility is to speak to the many rather than the few. Whether that's on a stage, a LinkedIn or Instagram Live, as a guest speaker on a podcast or hosting your own show, there is an amplified reach when speaking to a large audience. You have the potential to reach a significantly larger number of people compared to one-on-one interactions. This allows you to make a greater impact and spread your message to a broader audience.

One of the most important strategies is to capture and retain your audience's attention. With each speaking engagement, you have an opening to connect with hundreds or even thousands of individuals at once, exponentially increasing your reach. Many try and some fail. Work smart, not hard. A committed focus on those strategies means using your resources wisely which can lead to greater productivity and success. Effective hooks or props can open the minds of your audience, make them use their imaginations, trigger their senses and make them laugh, all of which can prove to be integrally persuasive and lighten the mood. It's the little things that make you stand out. Deseed the lemon.

Never underestimate the power of building a strong network when it comes to your personal brand strategy, whether that's actively speaking to people at networking events or speaking at conferences, industry events and seminars, live or virtual. It will help you to connect with like-minded individuals, industry leaders and potential collaborators. Building relationships with influential people in your field can open doors to new opportunities, partnerships and valuable connections that contribute to your personal brand growth.

I have seen the biggest results from public speaking when it allows you to connect with your audience on an emotional level. Sharing personal stories, experiences and insights can evoke emotions and leave a lasting impact. By connecting authentically, you build a loyal following and create emotional connections that strengthen your personal brand. People often think if they are in business, everything needs to be very dry and businesses focused, but quite the opposite. Emotionally connected individuals are more likely to remember your brand, develop loyalty and become brand advocates.

What's your napkin idea?

I can recall one of my early invitations to be a guest speaker at an event that was being held at the World Trade Centre, Dubai. I had been asked to share with delegates the story of my entrepreneurial journey. It was a very candid presentation about how I had pieced jigsaw pieces together to create an exciting new business concept, the first of its kind in the Middle East, and bring it to life.

How did this all happen? It was a Friday afternoon in April 2005, when I found myself sitting in a bar with one of my oldest friends who was on holiday. We were perched on a couple of bar stools by the waterside edge in the Madinat Jumeirah, Dubai's newest (at the time) hot spot for locals and tourists alike. I shared with my friend, Morven, something I had been mulling over for a while during down time when flying with Emirates – the first iteration of StyleMeDivine. The more I talked my idea over with Morven, the more I realised that I needed a plan.

Rummaging around in my bag, I found my pen, but to my dismay no paper. In front of me sat a pile of napkins. Taking one I proceeded to jot down, albeit somewhat roughly, my plan, lest I forget any detail. Fortunately, the napkin was not only a quality one, but also of a reasonable size. As I scribbled my thoughts legibly, I pronounced my plan was complete.

Whilst some of my best ideas come when I'm 30,000 feet up in the air, some other great ideas also come when I have a chilled glass of rosé wine in hand. It's all very well thinking about things, but if you really want to kick start your idea you need to write a plan, because something written becomes reality, it becomes your call to action.

Back to my talk at Dubai's World Trade Centre. As I shared my story with my audience and the process of how I had launched the Middle East's first personal shopping and styling business, I retrieved that same napkin and waved it around "Who here has a napkin idea?" I am at best enthusiastic about all aspects of my life, but this action generated quite a bit of interest. At my meet and greet with attendees following my presentation I found I had quite a queue waiting to speak to me to share their napkin ideas with me. It also gained me a few clients on that day.

Whilst facts and data alone can be forgettable, stories stick with people. When you present information in the form of a story, it becomes more memorable and relatable. Like props, stories provide context, vivid imagery and narrative structure that help your audience retain and recall the information you convey. This is particularly valuable in a business context where you want your message to be remembered and shared.

I host my own Kelly Lundberg podcast, as I mentioned in the previous chapter, and as a result I have met with well over 150 inspiring individuals from all professions and lifestyles. In episode 70, I interviewed Sanna Azzam, CEO & Chief Inspirational Officer of MENA Speakers, a leading speaker agency in the Middle East. She shared that the difference between a low-paid speaker and a highly-paid speaker is often a strong personal brand.

> "It's social proof that what you say is relevant and resonating with your audience. Often the bookings of these profiles are done by several people in an organisation and everyone runs their own diligence on the speaker. A personal brand makes it easier for every decision maker to feel comfortable in having that person influence an organisation and at times can be a choice for that organisation."

Everyone she accepts at MENA Speakers already has a strong personal brand.

Stories have the power to motivate individuals and by sharing moments of your journey overcoming challenges, achieving goals, or making a positive impact, you too can inspire your audience to act, pursue their own aspirations, or align with your business's vision. Motivated people are more likely to engage with your brand and become active participants in your success.

Stories have the power to build trust and credibility. When you share authentic and compelling stories, you create transparency and demonstrate your values, experiences and successes. My stories are calculated to share with you some small nuggets of information. They are life stories that may resonate with you to inspire you to elevate your personal brand and to remind you to deseed the lemon, one pip at a time.

It's important when you choose to share stories that you do not underestimate the crucial role they play in transmitting culture and values. This is particularly powerful within an organisational setting where you can instil a sense of identity and belonging among employees. At the heart of organisations cultural transmission fosters a positive work environment, strengthens morale and goes a long way to creating a cohesive work force.

Where to speak

You may just be starting out or are already a seasoned speaker, but want to increase your visibility and enhance your ability to attract fee-paying engagements. Either way, there are a vast number of lead-ins available for you to share your expertise and knowledge. Many conferences and events feature speaking slots for industry experts. If this is your goal, research conferences relevant to your field and reach out to organisers expressing your interest in speaking, share your speaker/media kit or submit a proposal.

Whilst some may ask you to speak for free to start with, as your experience grows you can expect to receive a speaker's fee. Valuable experience can be gained by participating in panel discussions at conferences, events, or webinars. When you engage in meaningful conversations with other industry experts, you will have the advantage of the exposure to showcase your expertise.

Another top tip is to join professional associations or networking groups related to your industry. These organisations often host events and invite members to speak on relevant topics. Quite recently I spoke to a women's networking group, free of charge, however, it converted into over $15,000 in sales post-event follow up.

Universities and colleges also are great stomping grounds to enquire about speaking at events such as career fairs, seminars, or as a guest lecturer to share your insights with students. I've regularly worked with a school in Dubai and one in Scotland with teenagers who were at the age where they were picking their GCSE subjects. Often, I am joined by their parents and we talk about not only subjects, but career paths too.

I didn't go to university to study a specific discipline; I chose to opt for the university of life; travel and work experience. I was always particularly keen to share my unconventional path with the teenagers I met and did this quite genuinely as I am passionate about inspiring the next generation. At one of those career seminars, it later transpired that a mum who had attended with her daughter went on to become one of my clients.

Look for platforms, collaborations and joint ventures that host webinars that attract your target audience where you can share value. These work the best when you have a clear call to action at the end of the presentation. Consider offering to conduct workshops or training sessions for companies, organisations, or educational institutions. This allows you to showcase your expertise while helping others learn valuable skills.

Post-pandemic virtual events, webinars and online masterclasses have become a popular way to share knowledge, build a database and grow your personal brand internationally. Many of my clients host their own events, webinars and masterclasses and achieve this successfully in the first few months of us working together.

Put yourself out there

Whilst public speaking can seem daunting, it does get easier and it's a learnable skill. I can still remember my first welcome meeting in Cyprus with a room full of eager holiday makers looking to me for information, and I promise the more you do it, the less scary it gets.

I worked with one client, Sara, who was petrified of public speaking. She was shy, felt totally exposed and was fearful of standing in front even just a small room of people. We focused specifically on her desire to increase her visibility, and confidence with her exposure. After speaking to a group, she sent me this voice note: "It was REALLY good! I had a mix of friends I know supporting so we were like eight or nine so it was a good session. Thank you very much, because if you did not push me I would not do it. I was so tired and so stressed. Thank you for being here."

Every personal brand strategy is unique to my clients. If they can do it, so can you.

Back in early 2015, one of my personal brand strategy goals was to give a TEDx talk, a more accessible option than a global TED talk, and something I knew Dubai hosted throughout the year. I knew that to deliver a talk at this level, it would push me to prepare and deliver a unique presentation, clearly articulate my ideas, refine my communication skills and overcome what was one of my biggest fears – to work without the use of cue cards or notes.

As a world-renowned platform, TED showcases ideas worth spreading, so an invitation to speak at a TED event or one of their community-led TEDx events, means you have credibility and positioning as an expert in your field. An association with TED and TEDx can elevate your reputation and make people take your ideas and expertise more seriously. As much as I was confident in my public speaking, I always had my comfort blanket of notes by my side. Not an option for the 12–18 minute format of a TEDx talk.

I had, at this point, no idea what my TEDx talk would be about, or if I would even be asked to deliver at some future point. The first thing I needed to do was carry out some research. I wanted to be ready for when, not if, the opportunity presented itself. Purchasing a copy of **Talk Like TED** by Carmine Gallo, public speaking coach and a bestselling author, I began my pursuit of knowledge (I told you I loved books!).

Gallo's book is "the book" for anyone who wants to speak with more confidence and authority. Breaking down the top TED talks, he interviewed the most popular TED presenters to uncover the nine secrets of all successful TED presentations. It will be your go-to if you are considering a TED or a TEDx talk as it shares some powerful ways to create and deliver an impactful presentation.

It was, to my surprise and great excitement, eight months later that a friend contacted me and said she was hosting TEDxJESS in Dubai and would I consider being a speaker. The theme was TIME. Jumeirah English Speaking School (JESS) is recognised as a truly international community with around 2,300 students, representing more than 70 different nationalities and speaking over 30 languages. It took just a nano second of time to give my response, a resounding yes.

When I read **Talk Like TED**, I learned that a scientist called Dr Jill Bolte Taylor gave one of the top TED talks of all time. To deliver, she had practised her entire talk some 200 times. I had five months to prepare my speech and practice delivering The Currency of Time TEDx talk. I was due to step on stage on 21 April 2016.

I took the practising element seriously and had a tally board of how many times I had practised rehearsing it – just like I had read, I wanted to get as close to 200 times as possible. Delivering a talk without notes terrified me. However, categorically one of the prerequisites of any TEDx talk is the ability to speak unaided by props for up to 18 minutes. At welcome meetings in my repping days, events, pitches and presentations in business I always had my notes as my safety blanket. Looking back, I can see that in some ways self-reliance on the use of notes held me back in my delivery and ability to connect in the moment.

By no means am I recommending freestyling your next presentation and just saying what comes off the top of your head. I still prepare with a few cue cards, but rarely use them. The delivery of my TEDx gave me the confidence to cut the cord. You don't need to be word perfect, your audience doesn't know what is coming next and you can always get back on track.

Many TEDx events choose speakers six months in advance, and the selection process means that you can go through two to four rounds of speaker selection. Being selected at the outset was quite an accolade. If you are considering delivering a TEDx talk as one of your goals, apply to any local event where you have a personal connection. It could be a city where you grew up, where your children go to school, or colleges or universities you attended.

Not every TEDx event requires speakers who live in the area. Some TEDx events specifically look for a wide mix of people with different talk styles and perspectives on life. I share my speaking experiences, which include being a TEDx Speaker, on my LinkedIn profile which has resulted in many and varied speaking opportunities from people searching for TEDx experience.

The business results of public speaking

I've been to see Steven Bartlett, entrepreneur, speaker, podcaster and author, present. One video he posted on LinkedIn unusually captured my eye as he shared that 70 per cent of his new business leads were coming through people who had watched him speak on stage or watched videos online and 70 per cent of the revenue that had reached his bank account had originated from some kind of personal brand initiative. Who doesn't want to increase their revenue by 70 per cent?

There is no doubt that public speaking is a valuable skill that extends beyond personal brand enhancement. It helps you develop your communication abilities, boost your confidence, and overcome any fear of public speaking. Think of my client Sara, who sent me that lovely and very personal voice note.

Public speaking challenges you to step out of your comfort zone and as you gain experience and improve your speaking skills, your confidence grows, just like me at TEDxJESS.

You can start right now by utilising platforms like Instagram, Facebook, or LinkedIn to host live sessions where you can share your expertise and engage with your followers directly, interview people or just share your real time moments. Go on, deseed the lemon, take the extra effort and host a webinar, a masterclass, a podcast, or just reach out and say hello live next week.

KEY PIP TAKEAWAYS

EMBRACE PUBLIC SPEAKING:

Recognise the power of speaking to a large audience to grow your personal brand credibility. Make a list of where you want to speak. Whether it's on a stage, through virtual platforms, or as a guest on podcasts, public speaking allows you to reach a broader audience and make a greater impact.

LEVERAGE SPEAKING ENGAGEMENTS FOR SOCIAL PROOF:

Seek speaking opportunities to showcase your expertise and share compelling presentations. Even if it means you are speaking for free to get visibility, awareness and photography content in the beginning, the exposure and validation you gain from speaking engagements can enhance your personal brand's reputation and credibility.

REPURPOSE CONTENT FROM SPEAKING ENGAGEMENTS:

Record and transcribe your presentations to create valuable content for various social platforms, blog posts, articles, or podcast episodes. Utilise this content to reach a wider audience and establish your expertise across different channels.

BUILD A STRONG NETWORK:

Actively participate in networking events, conferences and industry seminars to connect with like-minded individuals, industry leaders and potential collaborators. Tell people you speak so they know to hire you and make a list of places and events you can attend as part of your personal brand strategy.

CRAFT AND SHARE COMPELLING STORIES:

In your public speaking engagements, incorporate personal stories and experiences that evoke emotions and resonate with your audience. Emotional connections build trust, loyalty and a strong following, making your brand more memorable and relatable.

Chapter 15:

GETTING SPEAKING GIGS

Speaking engagements allow you to share unique insights, innovative ideas and industry trends. Combining this with excellent storytelling will help you to deliver thought-provoking presentations which can quickly position you as a thought leader in your field of expertise.

The way to ensure that you stand out from your competitors is by creating your very own Unique Personal Brand System or Solution (UPBS). A consistent framework that aligns with your knowledge, personal brand message and combines compelling stories can make the difference between someone choosing you over your competitor.

By developing your UPBS you can attract attention from media outlets, podcast hosts and industry publications, providing opportunities for interviews and features that further elevate your personal brand. Your UPBS can be an incredible asset within your personal brand equity as you can utilise it for sales conversations, the foundation for a book, as my system is, and in your marketing materials.

Having a UPBS helps not only organise information, but to visualise a process, and makes it easy for people who attend your event, presentation or hear your podcast to remember what was shared. It provides valuable content for your social media platforms building that essential foundation of trust and familiarity among your audience. When done with polish and perfection it makes it easier for an audience to engage with your content. It's your optimum moment to deseed the lemon.

Your UPBS is a high-level overview of how you help clients or colleagues to get the desired results and achieve their goals more quickly. A UPBS can be represented by a visual shape, for example a roadmap, a square, a circle or a triangle. Think of the pyramid shape of Maslow's Hierarchy of Needs, his model for understanding what motivates and fulfils humans. A tried-and-tested method should achieve this for you. You need to get the basics right! If you don't have the basics right you can't build anything that will last.

You may be thinking how this relates to your UPBS. Lou Stokes was one of my very early clients. She is a sustainability and fashion expert in Europe. As part of her personal brand strategy we created an acronym for her business system: I.C.O.N. (Inner world, Confidence, Own the skin you are in, New you).

I have adopted formulas that use alliteration, such as the 5 Cs, which you read about in Chapter 6, and the 6 Ps, which was part of my Magic Marketing Method in launching a personal styling business. Those 6 Ps were: Professional referrals, Personal referrals, Partnerships, Presenting, Press and Plan. I also used the acronym S.E.R.E.N.E Stylist, which was an easy way for stylists to remember Story, Elevator pitch, Rates, Executive summary, Niche and Experience. I mapped out this framework which became my 7 Steps Styling Formula, covering the seven steps aspiring stylists could implement to turn their passion for fashion into a profitable styling business.

Fashioning a tangible asset makes what you are offering more valuable. Plus with a structured approach, you demonstrate professionalism and expertise, leading to increased client satisfaction and loyalty. Your UPBS should, however, not be confused with systems and processes you already have within your business.

How to create your UPBS

When you create your UPBS you want to ultimately simplify your processes, the method you use to get results, with a high-level overview that is repeatable. So, how do you uncover your UPBS? First, you want to conduct research and engage in conversations with your clients to understand their pain points if you don't know them already – be clear about their challenges and goals. Identify the common problems they face and the outcomes they desire.

When I launched Brand YOU Creators, I created my own high-level overview framework, tailoring my approach after reaching out to my clients to understand their challenges. It was a Steve Jobs quote that resonated with me.

He said, "**You can't connect the dots looking forward; you can only connect them looking backwards.**" As I look back at the past 20 years of my entrepreneurial journey this rings true, the dots now start to join when I look at the subjective results of how I built my personal brand. Those big wins, the disappointment when things didn't quite gel and those awesome flukes all made sense. All of this culminated in the guiding principles for my personal branding solution.

With clear and specific objectives, like me, you can develop a guiding framework, your structured step-by-step process, that outlines the actions, strategies and tools required to address and achieve the desired outcomes for your clients. Processes can be broken down into bite-size chunks, giving you clear stages or modules. Look at the big picture and brainstorm first – don't get stuck in creating something that fits an acronym or alliteration straight away.

TOP TIP: HOW TO CREATE YOUR OWN UPBS

If you are struggling with how to compile your own system, start brainstorming. It gives you the opportunity to be creative, and to pull all the jumbled ideas from your head. Don't concern yourself with a "name" just yet, simply get all the steps onto paper.

Visualising the entire process will help, so place your objectives on a mind map. This visual representation will provide you with a holistic view of your system or formula. It will make it easier to evaluate whether your way of doing things is logical and coherent for someone encountering it for the first time.

By following this approach, you can ensure that your system is not only comprehensive, but also accessible and user-friendly, enhancing its effectiveness in solving the problem or achieving the desired outcome.

When you are ready with the flow, sprinkle in the magic by naming your system or formula. Make it memorable to stand out from the crowd – the catchier the better as long as it reflects your brand essence and attracts your ideal audience.

Be cognisant that your framework should be a dynamic tool that evolves with changing client needs and industry trends. Continuously gather feedback and analyse results to refine and improve your solutions over time. When I was working on my initial framework, I had to reassess the placement of my process structure to achieve a flow. I moved Style to the forefront of my framework, achieving the impact I desired. Your framework will vary from others. No two frameworks will look the same.

While your framework should have a structured process, it should also allow room for customisation to cater to individual client requirements. Not all clients will have the same requirements, so the ability to adapt the framework is essential. When it comes to my UPBS, some clients need more support with some areas than others and I tailor my approach accordingly.

Alongside the process, develop supporting resources such as templates, worksheets, guides and checklists to help clients implement the framework effectively. These resources can enhance the client's experience and increase the success of your solution. Develop marketing materials that clearly explain the benefits of your framework solution. This may include case studies, testimonials and success stories from clients who have experienced positive results using your framework.

You will also want to define specific metrics or key performance indicators (KPIs) to measure the success and effectiveness of your framework. This will enable you to track progress and showcase tangible results to your clients and/or colleagues. A well-designed framework solution not only helps your clients, but also sets your personal brand and business apart as a reliable and results-driven service provider. By providing a structured approach, you demonstrate high-quality detail, professionalism and expertise – it acts as the north star for everything you do.

The more you share your UPBS, the more doors will open for you to secure speaking opportunities. If you are asked to speak at an event you will find that companies, particularly corporate ones, like having a clear idea of the content you are going to deliver. You will need to think of yourself as a salesperson. Getting a speaking gig is a lot easier if you can provide examples of past successful speaking engagements and the value you have provided to other organisations. Show how your expertise can help the organisation achieve their objectives. It will go a long way to securing a booking, paid or otherwise.

Tips to promote your speaker profile and brand

Build on your personal brand equity by having a speaker kit or a professionally designed profile, as this will further enhance your personal brand. Speaker kits and media kits both serve distinct purposes in the realm of personal branding and public relations. A media kit, also known as a press kit or brand kit, is a comprehensive collection of resources and information that you provide to the media, potential collaborators, sponsors, or anyone interested in featuring you or your brand in their publications, interviews, or events. Its primary purpose is to make it easy for others to gather the necessary materials and information to accurately represent you.

Your typical media kit might include high-resolution images of you and an option to download more on a clickable link. It is a digital document. It may also include logos, branding elements and colours associated with your brand. A marketing team may need to know how to position your logo, or what specific colours you use. Whilst I personally don't put these into my media kit, you may choose to do so depending on your branding guidelines.

Your biography, usually written in the third person, should be brief and engaging. Best practice dictates that your bio should sit within your speaker/media kit and highlight your professional background, achievements and areas of expertise. I have taken an additional approach in my framework to write a personal welcome, while the rest remains written in the third person.

When including a description of your expertise, accomplishments and contributions, think about your achievements in measurable terms. For example, how many people have you inspired on a stage so far, can you work it out on average? It all evidences the value you can add. In my personal styling days, I used metrics like the number of personal shopping hours (15,000!), miles walked round malls and pairs of shoes purchased. Also link your social media profiles, along with any sample articles, interviews, or media coverage about you.

Finally, add testimonials or endorsements, brand logos of other organisations you have worked with for credibility and your contact information for inquiries, making sure it's a professional email address. Why not Gmail or Hotmail? Revisit Chapter 8 in Slice Three: Stationery.

Sometimes a speaker kit is referred to as a speaker one sheet. This is a subset of a media kit, essentially a one-pager or speaker's packet, specifically designed to promote individuals who are sought after to speak at conferences, events, workshops, or webinars. It's geared towards event organisers and conference planners to help them understand your speaking topics, style, and once again endorse the value you can bring to their event.

In addition to your speaker bio and headshot, you will want a detailed list of speaking topics and descriptors. Share an overview of previous speaking engagements and events and link to your showreel, if you have one, or any video clips of past presentations. If you have any published works or books, or relevant certifications or credentials, these all add weight to your speaker/media kit.

Style of delivery varies from individual to individual. My style tends to be very expressive and handsfree, having perfected the art of not needing cue cards and notes from my TEDx days. Depending on your niche, you might need to add a section about technical requirements for your speaking engagements, such as any AV equipment needed. I don't share this at this stage, however, I request prior to the event that the mic is a lapel mic rather than handheld, unless it's a panel discussion.

With a speaker/media kit, you can easily share your information with event organisers, conference planners, or clients. It's a great central point of all information that interested parties will need so that they can contact you for future bookings. Whether it's through email, digital platforms, or in-person meetings, having a comprehensive package readily available makes it convenient to provide all the necessary details in a professional manner. You will save time and effort by having a speaker kit readily available when responding to inquiries or requests for information.

Sharing a well-crafted media or speaker kit demonstrates professionalism and shows that you take your personal brand and speaking engagements seriously. Your efforts here are all part of you deseeding the lemon. A speaker kit also allows you to maintain a unified message and image across different platforms and interactions, ensuring that everyone receives consistent and accurate information about your speaking services.

Overall, a speaker/media kit is an invaluable tool for promoting yourself as a speaker. For maximum impact, combine this with your UPBS showcasing your expertise. When you facilitate effective communication with event organisers and clients, you will create a positive and lasting impression, ultimately increasing your chances of securing speaking opportunities, and building a successful speaking career.

KEY PIP TAKEAWAYS

CREATE YOUR OWN UNIQUE PERSONAL BRAND SYSTEM OR SOLUTION (UPBS):

Develop a consistent framework that aligns with your knowledge and personal brand message. This framework should combine compelling stories and practical strategies.

CREATE A COMPREHENSIVE SPEAKER/MEDIA KIT:

The idea is that anyone visiting your kit can figure out the essential information about who you are and what your business is. You can then tailor this for event organisers and conference planners who are seeking speakers. The key is to make it easy to update, easy to share and easy to adapt. Have a list of potential speaking topics you can talk about, including panel discussion. Create a one-page speaker profile so you can send it to speaking agencies, events companies and corporate companies.

SHARE YOUR UPBS CONSISTENTLY IN YOUR CONTENT AND PRESENTATIONS:

Consistent content establishes authority and credibility. Your UPBS not only organises your expertise, but also acts as a visual and memorable process for your audience.

Deseed The Lemon

SLICE SEVEN:

STAND OUT

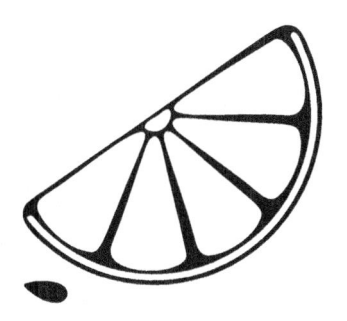

You have invested time, thought and effort in the creation of your personal brand strategy. You've approached it slice by slice, deseeding each segment pip by pip.

However, to stand out goes way beyond delivering amazing customer service. This is how you connect authentically and communicate your uniqueness effectively.

This final slice is where you can make the difference when you deseed the lemon. Go the extra mile that others aren't and leave a lasting impression. In doing so, you're ensuring that your personal brand not only resonates with your audience, but also thrives in a world filled with competition.

The internet and social media are amazing tools for helping us be seen and building our personal brands, but they also mean we are now competing with more people than ever before. When you commit to showing up as the best version of yourself every day, you will begin to stand out more and more. It all comes back to consistency – if you can consistently show up for your ideal audience, be authentic and share valuable content, you'll see your personal brand start to rise.

You need to deseed the lemon here, otherwise you run the risk of putting out generic content that gets lost in the noise. So, it's time to tap into your uniqueness and make sure you're communicating that loud and clear with your ideal audience.

Chapter 16:

WAYS TO STAND OUT FROM EVERYONE ELSE

Your personal brand is a clear reflection of what already exists inside of you, you don't have to manufacture it. What characteristics you choose to project as your compelling personal brand to stand out is a culmination of many things executed consistently.

Know what your strengths and weaknesses are. It's vital that you know both. It's often easier to concentrate on what you are good at, but it is just as important that you recognise areas of weakness and take note. Own what you are not so good at, because you will be able to build a stronger personal brand if you can be honest about things you are insecure about. People are very often more willing to trust you.

Creating a compelling personal brand, if you do it well, can take you anywhere you want to go. Your personal brand is an expression of your lifestyle, what you are about, your goals and where your journey is headed. If your brand is authentic, people will follow, like and know you. A distinct and compelling personal brand is truly what leaves a remarkable imprint on someone forever.

A personal brand is not about being perfect – be real and show your human side. It's not about self-promotion either. Bragging is neither sophisticated nor subtle. Remember a strong personal brand is all about being genuine. Nor is it all about competition, be the best version of yourself, there is no gain in trying to outdo competitors. Don't follow trends, stay true to yourself and your values that you have worked so hard to define.

How can you stand out? Aim to show up as the best version of yourself every day.

Some of you may not wish to stand out, maybe you feel uncomfortable with the spotlight aimed right at you. There are, however, all kinds of approaches where you can thrive and stand out without being that person in the spotlight. Some may want to be up on a stage to thank someone or collect an award that they have been nominated for, some may quietly choose to shine a light on sustainable charitable causes.

The power of a simple gesture

What you say and do matter greatly when it comes to carving out your personal brand. By taking charge of your personal brand, you can direct how others think and feel when they interact with you. I like to send handwritten notes to my clients, to friends and to family. This can be construed as old school and an outdated mode of communication, not to mention the environmental factor when we are all trying to reduce our carbon footprint. We all say thank you, or at least we think we do. But how well do we really do this simple yet powerful act? Have you considered this as part of your personal brand?

The ease of technology often means reverting to sending a quick text message, a WhatsApp notification, or an email and always from your personal branded email. These do have a place. However, consider the impact that you could make if you went the extra mile, if you actively deseeded the lemon by taking time to focus on the smaller details, making that extra effort, going above and beyond and expressing your recognition with a handwritten note. Written communication conveys an appreciation for someone in your life. In my experience it's a surefire way to make your personal brand stand out.

Expressing gratitude by writing down your thanks can be good for you. In a brain scanning study published in **NeuroImage** the effects of gratitude expression on neural activity were examined. It was found that even months after a simple, short gratitude writing task, people's brains are still wired to feel extra thankful.[15] The more you practise gratitude, the more attuned you are to it and the more you can enjoy its psychological benefits. Scientists

---

15 Kini, P. et al. (2016) 'The effects of gratitude expression on neural activity,' NeuroImage, 128, pp. 1–10. https://doi.org/10.1016/j.neuroimage.2015.12.040.

who have studied written gratitude interventions, such as letters of thanks or gratitude journals, believe there are direct benefits for your mental health and wellbeing.

It was a New Year's tradition in our household to handwrite thank you letters. As soon as we were old enough to put together a few sentences legibly my sister and I were to be found sitting at the kitchen table, pens in hand to write thank yous for our Christmas gifts. It was a tradition that my granny had passed to my mum, and my mum made sure we did it too. Early signs of deseeding the lemon.

Miraculously, Santa never ever forgot to leave us well prepared, placing a suitable packet of thank you cards in our stockings. I think we would have been around the age of nine or ten. Quite honestly, I can share with you it was a tradition that I disliked intensely and dreaded having to do. That was then!

Every year, my sister and I would have the same argument with mum. We moaned incessantly trying to put off the moment of pain, Christmas was holiday time, fun time. We wanted to be out riding on our new bikes or playing with our dolls, not pouring over thank you cards.

My mum would have none of that, writing our thank you cards was, she insisted, non-negotiable and a simple exercise in good manners. As the elder sister, I dared to challenge her, asking why exactly we had to. Her explanation was pretty simple, she said that we needed to be thankful for all the gifts we had received and recognise the effort others put in on our behalf.

That lesson, and tradition, has stayed with me. Writing thank you notes has become a habit that I enjoy and I take great pleasure in sending thank you cards where recognition is deserved. It makes me happy and my mum even more so. I just wish my granny was still with me to see the results of this activity and the delight of those who receive my notes.

Who would have known that some 30 years later, I would be sending handwritten thank you cards to brands like Chanel, Louis Vuitton and Harvey Nichols to express my gratitude for being invited to work on a project with their staff. I genuinely believe that the personal approach opens the door to newer or greater friendships and business relationships.

Did you forget something?

My friends and family are among my fellow lemon deseeders in their own rights. Yvonne and Sarah are two of my very best friends. Sarah still resides in Dubai and as a highly successful event planner, her attention to detail is second to none. She consummately deseeds the lemon. Yvonne left Dubai several years ago and settled back in her home country, Scotland. Ours is a friendship that spans 20 years and despite our different locations, we made a pact that we would catch up annually no matter where we were in the world, to spend some quality time together. We fondly named our threesome "The VC Club", founded on our love for champagne, Veuve Clicquot.

Through thick or thin we have consistently committed to meeting up. We've seen marriages and divorce, boom and bust, relocations, job changes and a global pandemic. I can happily report that we have stuck to our pact, aside from the pandemic throwing us, like many others, out of sync. To date we have chalked up trips to Bali, New York, Paris, Crete, London, and a fair few to France and one to Budapest. Each trip has been our opportunity to reconnect and find out what's going on in one another's lives.

During one of our trips, I listened with fascination as Yvonne shared stories of guests who booked to stay at her castle. Yvonne and her husband had, on their return to Scotland, bought Turin Castle, which they turned into a luxury venue for exclusive hire. No surprise there, considering that Yvonne is an amazing host – and I should know, having enjoyed her awesome hospitality on many occasions both when she lived in Dubai and at her new home at Turin. Nothing is ever too much trouble for Yvonne to organise; she goes out of her way to make each person's stay with her special as well as unforgettable. I can't wait for 2024, as Turin Castle is going to be the venue for my Scottish wedding.

Always discreet, protecting her clients' anonymity, we listened raptly as Yvonne shared a story about a particular group of guests who had hired her venue. An all-American party of gents were preparing to leave. Their stay had been, in their own words, "memorable and perfect in every way". Always one with an eye for detail, as they made their final preparations Yvonne thought to ask if they had everything they needed before they headed home. Equivocally, they all nodded enthusiastically declaring that their packing was complete. Yvonne was less than sure, asking them whether they had remembered holiday gifts for their spouses and children. Crestfallen, the gents quickly realised the error of their ways until Yvonne directed their attention to neatly wrapped parcels at the front door.

In the week these guests had stayed with Yvonne, she had listened carefully and taken notes. Yvonne excels at deseeding the lemon, and she had made a list of who was who and, checking with each of the gents' personal assistants, she weaved her Scottish magic, purchasing and packing Scottish cashmere blankets for the ladies and Scottish storybooks for the children. Each parcel was personally tagged, awaiting collection.

I've since heard that on their arrival back in the United States, this action generated serious interest in a further substantial order of cashmere blankets. Sourced once again by a skilful Yvonne, she is not only yet again deseeding the lemon, but building her personal brand and business to make her stand out from her competitors. A personal brand that resonates emotionally with your clients and audience on social media forms a deeper connection. Emotions are a powerful driving force for engagement and long-term loyalty.

Further evidence of how deseeding the lemon can transcend happened last year when I took my mum to W The Palm Jumeirah in Dubai for her birthday treat. Like the VC girls, me and mum love quality time together and as an expat it's always quality over quantity. I had let The W know we were celebrating a special birthday, a big number, can't say which one for fear she will kill me!

At check in we were upgraded and offered early entry to our room. It didn't take us long to drop off our bags, change into our swimsuits and head to the pool to chill. Returning to the room and opening the door, my jaw dropped. Inside was a sea of helium balloons floating on the ceiling, each with a string and a photo attached to them. There were photographs of my family, my sister, my stepdad, grandsons, many pictures from our adventures together and a cake with a personal message for her birthday.

I found out that a member of the PR team had diligently gone through both my Instagram and my mum's choosing pictures to mark her life and travels. They had effectively deseeded the lemon. It was completely unexpected and the memories that it made have been lasting, mum still talks about this experience and how special it made her feel.

Looking to recreate this moment, a few months later I had a friend who was celebrating his 40th birthday in Los Angeles. He would be staying in the W Los Angeles – West Beverly Hills. Perfect I thought, let's make the magic happen again. I managed, although not with the greatest of ease, to track down someone who said they could help me with a similar surprise. My first red flag. Sharing images of mum's experience in Dubai and my desire to recreate the same wow factor, I was assured everything would be arranged. I sent some pictures I had of my friend to attach to the balloons and was excited to receive the feedback of his surprise experience.

Consistency it seems is not something that was applied. When we look to stand out it comes down to personal brand and not just the company brand. I spent two days trying to track down my contact who had assured me that all things were possible. I tried by telephone, WhatsApp, and email, only to be ghosted. Hence my red flag! The result was lacklustre. My friend's partner shared the context of my birthday surprise: four children's balloons placed on the TV console. That was it – two 5-star hotels, under the same company brand, but the experience was very different. Why? The evidence, plain to see, was down to an individual's personal brand, the value that they wanted to add and their overriding desire to unconsciously deseed the lemon. It would have been far easier if the person I spoke to had said, "Sorry we don't offer that here, but we can do X or Y," and thereby personalised in their own way.

So what makes the difference between a stand out experience and one that leaves you feeling less than enthused?

When dining recently at the newly renovated Nobu, Atlantis the Palm, I asked to speak to the manager. My husband and I had enjoyed an exceptional dining experience in every sense for the second time – the welcome, the food, the customer service, the wine, everything was perfect, we could fault nothing and only compliment all. I was interested to understand how his restaurant was able to stand out from all the other Nobus around the world.

The manager's belief is that you can easily have the same person eating the same dish in two different restaurants made from identical recipes. What makes the difference is the people who take the time to understand the diners' needs. The vibe of every restaurant can differ, and at Nobu, Atlantis the Palm their secret was to listen to conversations unobtrusively to remember how someone likes their wine poured, their drink mixed, where they like to sit and if they have been to the restaurant before. Their aim is to know their client, and to understand and achieve their clients' expectations thus creating a lasting memory that people will talk about, share, and return for again and again.

Employers can be very nervous about investing in employees' personal brands. In an article I wrote for **Arabian Business** I shared several reasons why investing in employee brands can have a profound impact on the overall business.[16]

"YOUR TEAM ARE YOUR BRAND AMBASSADORS AND PEOPLE WANT TO ENGAGE WITH PEOPLE RATHER THAN BUSINESSES. REAL LIFE, BEHIND-THE-SCENES STORIES, HUMAN CONNECTION, AND RELATIONSHIPS, BUILD A MUCH LONGER LASTING BOND WITH CONSUMERS."

---

16   ICP, (2021), 'Why you should be investing in your employees' personal brand', *Arabian Business*, 6 Sept, available at: https://www.arabianbusiness.com/opinion/comment/468035-why-you-should-be-investing-in-your-employees-personal-brand

"THE CHANCES OF A BUSINESS BEING COMPLETELY UNIQUE AND NICHE IS RARE THESE DAYS WHICH MEANS THERE IS ALWAYS COMPETITION, A NEW KID ON THE BLOCK. YES, YOU CAN TRY AND BEAT YOUR COMPETITORS ON PRICE, BUT WITHOUT A BRAND AND PERSONAL CONNECTION, YOU BECOME A COMMODITY THAT COMPETES ONLY ON PRICE. THERE IS IMPROVED VISUAL AND VOICE CONNECTION, AND INCREASED EMPLOYEE RETENTION AS YOU ENCOURAGE EMPLOYEES TO DEVELOP THEIR PERSONAL BRAND. IT HELPS THEM GROW WITHIN THEIR OWN CAREERS AND BECOME MORE ACCOUNTABLE."

And the winner is…

Nominations for an award within a company or externally are excellent ways in which to stand out. Awards have a lasting impact and even if you don't win, the process of either applying or attending a ceremony that you were nominated for can prompt you to evaluate your achievements, set more goals and refine your personal brand strategy, as was the case for one of my clients in Houston, Texas, Krista Satterthwaite, who is Senior Vice President and General Manager for Compute at Hewlett

Packard Enterprise. She is the recent recipient of three awards "50 Women to Watch for Boards 2023", "BPTN Black Tech Executive of The Year 2023" and "Savoy 2019 Most Influential Women in Corporate America".

These accolades prompted her to look at her personal brand within the business and create a strategy around how she could mentor and inspire others within the organisation, in addition to performing her core role. She now organises group mentoring, shares books that have helped her on her career journey, speaks on numerous panels and presents keynotes, all under her personal brand.

It can take time to get noticed and to be nominated for awards. In some instances, you may need to put yourself forward. The first award ceremony I ever attended in business was held by Lloyds TSB Banking group. For several years, they celebrated small and medium-sized enterprises (SMEs) in Dubai, bringing them all together at an annual awards ceremony. Attending as a new business owner I loved being surrounded by so many businesses and founders. Inspired by their success I was very curious to know how you win one of these coveted awards. As the ceremony drew to a close, I chose my moment to stand out.

Approaching the gentleman who had closed off the event, I naively asked, "How do you win one of these awards?" He enthusiastically shared with me that applications for next year's awards would open in three months' time. The criteria for registration was a business with a gross revenue over a certain amount, with the application process involving interviews held by a judging panel. Determined that I would be on stage next year collecting an award, I had clarity over my goal.

Over the next 12 months I made sure my business grew to reach the required revenue, and attended the interviews with the judging panel. They were no walk in the park, and I found them challenging, thought provoking and demanding. On awards day I found out that I was nominated in three of the eight categories.

I was elated, and a little intimidated. My styling business was a new concept in the Middle East and I felt very conspicuous as the room of over 300 people all gathered to hear who the winners and losers would be. As the master of ceremonies read out my name as the winner of the creative promotion award, I could hardly believe my ears. I had set out my goal with absolute clarity and achieved it within my set time frame.

With my hands shaking, I stood on stage to give my acceptance speech – it was like my own pinch me version of the Oscars, minus the glamorous gown. It was, after all, only 8am. The bright stage lights made me hot and sweaty; I was praying that my newly purchased Dianne Von Furstenberg printed blouse was not showing me up. I remember saying, "Wow if I could bottle up this feeling and sell it, maybe next year I'd win the overall business award." Everyone laughed and I relaxed.

Starting a business can be a very lonely world, especially if you have come from a corporate environment and bigger teams. Being recognised with an award can boost your confidence and self-esteem. The external validation can confirm you are on the right track and doing the right thing, which helped inspire me immensely at 26 years old.

Unknown to me at the time, there were so many benefits to winning an award apart from the external validation of my skills, expertise and contributions to the industry. The recognition enhanced my personal brand's reputation and set me apart as a trusted and respected entrepreneur. There was a lot of media coverage and many press releases went out. As part of my prize there were three days of adverts in the local paper. This was in the days before social media! Nowadays winning an award can increase your visibility very quickly, attracting new opportunities, followers and potential clients or partners.

Award ceremonies and events offer excellent networking opportunities. I connected with fellow nominees, winners, judges and industry professionals, all of whom can lead to valuable relationships and partnerships. One of those partnerships led to another excellent way to stand out and deseed the lemon: writing a book.

Despite this being my second published book, I am no writer and consider myself much more of a talker. However, in 2009 my Lloyds TSB award spawned my idea to write **Success in the City: Dubai Entrepreneurs Tell Their Story**. Inspired, I knew I wanted to share other entrepreneurs' journeys. I also wanted to prove my high school teacher wrong – the one who told me in senior year that I would never achieve my higher-grade English.

My plan was to self-publish 3,000 copies of my book. However, to do this I needed support with costs. What better idea than approaching Lloyds TSB Bank to be my sponsor. I positioned my book idea as a gift they could share with new business banking clients about the vision of entrepreneurs in Dubai, showing that anything is possible with the right mindset, they agreed.

Incorporating a book into your personal brand strategy requires dedication, time and effort, which is why I believe it is where you can deseed the lemon. It's an investment that not only enhances your brand's influence, but also provides a platform to share your knowledge and leave a lasting impact. I quickly realised that publishing a book was not a massive revenue stream, despite my world domination plans of launching a **Success in The City** book in every city, but what it did do was elevate my visibility.

It opened doors to speaking engagements and media features, and as a result generated a much higher revenue stream. That's not to say you can't be the next J.K. Rowling and as much as I tried to glean inspiration when I returned to Edinburgh, visiting the cafes where she wrote **Harry Potter**, my best ideas still come when I am 30,000 feet in the sky.

There are many advantages to publishing a book as a business or thought leader in addition to this increased visibility, as Georgia Kirke, Founder of Write Business Results, explains.

"When I think of all the business events I've been to, perhaps ever, but certainly in the last five years, at least 90 per cent of the speakers are also published authors. On a personal level, when I need to update my knowledge on any area of business, books are the first resource I turn to.

To me it seems completely natural that any person who's leading a business should be able to package up who they are, what they do, what they know, their personal experiences and their stories in the form of a book. The reason is that this is how you become established – you don't become known as an expert and then write the book later, the book is what makes you the expert. It gets your name out there, it makes you the go-to and it gives you a one-to-many platform versus just one-to-one.

What's really important with a book is that you're taking the time to demonstrate your knowledge and expertise, because ultimately if you don't take ownership of your niche, your competitors will.

There is a big opportunity to being a published author in terms of leverage. A book is more than a piece of marketing or content. You can leverage your book to access more speaking gigs, open new conversations with higher-level people and form strategic partnerships. You can even use your book to leverage the exit of your company and a couple of my clients have done exactly that.

The most typical result from becoming a published author is making additional six figures by using the book

> for lead generation and thought leadership. This comes in the form of speaking gigs at the top of your funnel, lead generation as people go through your marketing funnel, lead nurture as people go through the sales process and even as a referral tool. You can use your book to nurture your existing clients and then create new business opportunities with them, such as through upsells. People will pay more to work with an expert they can trust and, as a published author, you're positioning yourself as that expert and can therefore legitimately increase your fees."

Give to get

Over the years I have invested significantly in personal development and continuous learning as part of my personal brand journey. My goal is always to share what I learn with clients and continue to keep up with market trends. From London to Los Angeles, I have attended conferences, workshops, training and one of those events was "Tony Robbins, A Date with Destiny".

One of the many experiences he shared was that the secret to living is giving – he even made this his last chapter in **Money Master the Game: 7 Simple Steps to Financial Freedom**.[17] He revealed that the ultimate goal for attaining financial freedom is to have the opportunity to give

---

17   Robbins T., (2026), 'Money Master the Game: 7 Simple Steps to Financial Freedom', *Simon & Schuster UK*

and that is something that is really close to my heart and personal brand. Supporting causes creates a positive impact on society or the environment, or both. This aligns your personal brand with a sense of purpose and responsibility, it also shows that you're not just focused on self-promotion, but also making a difference.

Taking a stand for causes inspires others to do the same. Your personal brand becomes a source of influence, motivating others to support meaningful initiatives. Whether you choose to talk about what causes you support is an entirely personal decision, however, with a public profile I can use my platforms to inspire others where I can.

With strict laws, supporting charities historically in the United Arab Emirates (UAE) proved challenging. Charities can only be permitted if approved by the relevant authority and registered charities in the UAE need a specific permit to allow them to collect donations. I launched the giving back style bangle, which meant all profits went to an orphanage in Thailand I had visited previously. My personal brand supported school uniforms for children in Dhaka, Bangladesh, but I had a burning desire to do more. All that changed the day I met Sarah Brook, founder of The Sparkle Foundation in Malawi.

I talked about how she was a guest on my podcast in Chapter 13, and as well as volunteering in person in Malawi, I was able to connect with her cause and champion it in Dubai, because it officially had a licence to operate as a charity in the UAE.

Being able to help children means so much to me. For you it might be rescuing cats or dogs, protecting the ocean, or finding a cure for cancer or motor neurone disease – around the world there are so many initiatives to support those that are not as fortunate as we are. Aligning with causes you care about showcases your authenticity. It demonstrates that your personal brand is grounded in genuine values and principles, making your brand more relatable and trustworthy.

When your personal brand is associated with causes that resonate emotionally, it deepens the connection you have with your audience, fostering loyalty and engagement. When I visited Malawi in 2022, I was conscious that I was able to engage with more people on a much deeper and much more personal level. I received many generous donations to take with me and was able to shine the light on Sarah's efforts over the past ten years, allowing her to stand out.

Taking a stand for causes inspires others to do the same, motivating others to support meaningful initiatives. In an era where social responsibility is valued, actively supporting causes highlights your commitment to being a responsible global citizen. Integrating causes that matter into your personal brand narrative not only contributes to a better world, but also enhances your personal brand's appeal and impact. It's a meaningful way to differentiate yourself, connect with your audience on a deeper level, and leave a positive mark on both your industry and society as a whole.

Where every detail and choice matters, the concept of deseeding the lemon takes centre stage. This process outlined in the Seven Slices: Strategy, Style, Stationery, Social, Spotlight, Speaking and Stand Out involves the accumulation of seemingly minor decisions, actions and characteristics that, when combined, shape a distinctive and compelling personal brand. This deliberate effort leaves an indelible mark on the lives of those touched by it. The art of crafting a personal brand is where you truly have the opportunity to shine.

Perhaps some readers of this book may hold reservations about standing out, concerned that self-promotion might overshadow their values. However, within these pages, you've discovered strategies that allow you to stand out in an elegant and understated manner. By showcasing sustainable and charitable endeavours, expressing gratitude, or receiving recognition, you create a magnetic allure that entices others to explore and engage with your personal brand.

More than skin deep

Remember, your personal brand extends beyond mere perception. It resonates deeply with others through the emotions you evoke when they encounter your words and actions. These words and actions range from sharing your opinions on stage or via a social media post, to the impact of a handwritten note in today's digital age, or going the extra mile to leave a lasting impression on your customers or colleagues. It's these small, thoughtful gestures that can elevate your personal brand and set you apart.

Investing in your personal brand doesn't solely entail accolades and awards. It's a continuous pursuit of growth and refinement, a journey where personal development takes centre stage. By embracing this path, you not only enhance your own brand, but also create a positive ripple effect in the lives of those you touch.

Unveiling the potential within your personal brand sometimes calls for you to explore uncharted territory. Writing a book, for instance, demands dedication and effort, yet it offers a unique platform through which to share your knowledge and leave a legacy. Beyond elevating your brand's influence, a book invites readers into your world, strengthening connections and sparking meaningful conversations.

In fact, these actions are not merely about differentiation; they hold the power to foster lasting connections and relationships. Just as the art of deseeding a lemon is in the meticulous care taken, nurturing your personal brand involves cultivating authentic interactions and genuine connections. It's about creating a sense of belonging and emotional resonance that draws people closer. Whether you are smart, unconventional, left field or quirky, let your unique light shine. There is no one quite like you!

KEY PIP TAKEAWAYS

BE REAL AND NOT PERFECT:

Your personal brand isn't about self-promotion or competition. It's about being genuine, showing your human side, and staying true to your values.

THE POWER OF PERSONAL GESTURES:

Small, thoughtful actions, like sending handwritten notes, can have a significant impact on your personal brand. They convey appreciation and create a lasting impression.

Ways to Stand Out from Everyone Else

YOUR PERSONAL BRAND EXTENDS BEYOND PERCEPTION:

Emotions you evoke in others through words and actions, including small, thoughtful gestures, will set you apart.

SUPPORTING CAUSES:

Aligning your personal brand with causes you care about demonstrates authenticity and social responsibility. It serves to deepen your connection with your audience and motivates others to support meaningful initiatives.

EMBRACE YOUR UNIQUENESS:

Let your unique light shine.
Be yourself – there is no one quite like you.

Deseed The Lemon

~ THE END ~

CONCLUSION

Each of the Seven Slices I have shared with you encapsulates the potential to forge a more refined and enriched version of yourself, elevating your personal brand. To recap, these Seven Slices are:

SLICE ONE: STRATEGY

You need a clearly defined strategy to build a successful personal brand. This means you need to know where you're starting from, what your values are and what your goals are. When you have these foundations in place, you can create a plan to follow and will be able to clearly articulate your message in the form of an elevator pitch. All of this will ensure consistency as you build your personal brand.

SLICE TWO: STYLE

Your style is about far more than what you wear (although this is important), it's how you express yourself to the world. It encompasses your clothes, accessories, makeup and how you communicate and interact with others. Your personal style reflects your identity and it's important that this comes across from the first time someone meets you. After all, first impressions count.

SLICE THREE: STATIONERY

Stationery refers to all the collateral touchpoints that represent your personal brand. This covers everything from brochures and ebooks to your website and photography. It's your visual identity. Well-designed brand collateral will get you noticed and strengthen the bond between you and your clients. To ensure consistency with your visual identity, make sure you create clear personal brand guidelines early on.

SLICE FOUR: SOCIAL

Social media is just one part of your digital presence, but it's an important one. It's important to take a strategic view of your social media activity and make sure you are focusing on the platforms and mediums that best resonate with your target audience. You need to be authentic on social media, and keep your content fresh and engaging. Also remember that social media algorithms are constantly evolving, so it pays to monitor your content's performance and experiment with different strategies.

Conclusion

SLICE FIVE: SPOTLIGHT

Gaining media coverage will put you firmly in the spotlight and in doing so can both establish and enhance your personal brand credibility. This is a great opportunity to share your unique story with a wider audience, as well as to publish thought leadership content that positions you as an expert. Network and engage wherever you can, always putting the focus on building relationships, whether that's with journalists or your target audience.

SLICE SIX: SPEAKING

Public speaking is one of the best ways to share your message and knowledge in a one-to-many format. What's more, speaking in front of large audiences further validates your expertise and personal brand credibility. You can also create valuable content from speaking opportunities, which can be repurposed for your social media, blog, YouTube channel or podcast. Creating a Unique Personal Brand System or Solution can help ensure consistency of messaging and make your presentations visual and memorable for your audience.

SLICE SEVEN: STAND OUT

This final slice is all about going the extra mile to leave a lasting impression and connect with your audience in a unique and meaningful way. This is the epitome of deseeding the lemon and when you do this well, you will stand out even in a world full of competition. Embrace your uniqueness and show people who you are as a person. Don't underestimate the power of personal gestures or the importance of aligning your personal brand with causes you care about.

To deseed the lemon goes beyond the metaphor; it's a mindset that permeates every facet of your personal brand. If you choose to lead through example, you can illuminate the path towards personal growth and transformation. This will only come if you make the call to action.

A competitive and dynamic world will require you to stand out and resonate with others who share your authenticity. How you present yourself, your skills, your values and your goals – both on and off line – are the threads to weave into the tapestry of your personal brand.

It's not just about how you appear to others; it's about how you make them feel, connecting them to you with tangible emotions that leave an indelible and enduring mark.

Share your own stories, especially those moments when you've witnessed or have experienced someone who deseeds the lemon. These instances of meticulous attention and effort serve to remind us that true greatness is composed of those small, deliberate acts that inspire others and shape our collective journey towards a brighter future.

Look out for someone who has a story like Sarah Brook from Sparkle, or my friend Yvonne from Turin Castle who offers exceptional service. Tag @deseedthelemon, let's start to build a community of deseeders!

Conclusion

How was your hot water and lemon, was it full of pips? My granny will surely be looking down from one of her many heavenly tea parties, softly saying, "Nothing worse than a few floating pips…"

You will no doubt have realised where you can deseed the lemon and remove the pips from the experiences and interactions you have with others after reading this book and learning about my Seven Slices for success. It's my desire that you not only apply what you've learned to building your personal brand and growing your business, but also to your personal life and relationships. As we all know deep down, a little extra effort and care goes a long way. I've compiled some resources to help you on your journey to deseed the lemon. You'll find them here: **Deseedthelemon.com.**

One-to-one session
Kelly and her team at Brand YOU Creators can support you with your personal brand journey whether you're an entrepreneur, employee, CEO, or sports person, with a complete personal brand strategy, design, and delivery. For more information visit: www.kellylundbergofficial.com

Corporate workshop
Want to bring the power of personal branding to your organisation? Kelly regularly hosts keynotes and training for teams, organisations and events. For more information and to watch videos from her previous workshops, visit www.brandyoucreators.com

Deseed The Lemon

Please reach out, I would love to hear your stories and to meet you!

ABOUT THE AUTHOR

Kelly Lundberg is a bestselling author and multi-award-winning entrepreneur. The former celebrity stylist currently hosts her own top-rated podcast delivering on her mission to inspire at least five people a day to take action to improve their personal brand.

Although she's based in Dubai, Kelly is proudly Scottish and shares her stories, knowledge and experience as a TEDx speaker, Personal Brand Strategist and Business Mentor. She works globally with CEOs, entrepreneurs and some of the biggest retail and luxury brands worldwide, helping them to elevate their personal brand to maximise income and impact.

A keynote speaker, Kelly hosts events and delivers motivational sessions across the world on entrepreneurship and personal branding. As a self-appointed member of the "5AM Club", you'll often find Kelly working out by the beach at sunrise. She has a loyal social media following, with whom she shares her style, sundowners and authentic business tips.

Printed in Great Britain
by Amazon